ADA CARTIANU

THE ALCHEMY OF *Self-Discovery*

A QUEST FOR AN AUTHENTIC EXISTENCE
EMBRACE THE MESSY, BEAUTIFUL PROCESS
OF BECOMING OUR TRUEST SELVES

RebELLE Publishing Agency
Printed in the United States of America

THE ALCHEMY OF SELF-DISCOVERY
A QUEST FOR AN AUTHENTIC EXISTENCE
EMBRACE THE MESSY, BEAUTIFUL PROCESS
OF BECOMING OUR TRUEST SELVES

TABLE OF CONTENTS

10 **The Uncomfortable Truth: Confronting the Gap Between Expectation and Reality**
    Unmasking Societal Expectations
16 Identifying Your Internal Conflicts
21 Recognizing Symptoms of Disconnection
27 Unveiling Your Inner World
32 Embracing Vulnerability:
A Path to Authenticity

37 **Understanding Your Values: The Compass of Your Soul**
    Understanding Core Values
43 Values Clarification Exercise
48 Aligning Actions with Values
53 Values as a Guide to Making Decisions
58 Redefining Success Beyond External Validation

63 **Discovering Your Passions: Ignite Your Inner Fire**
    Uncovering Different Talents and Interests
68 Exploring Creative Outlets
72 Turning Passion into Purpose
77 Overcoming Limiting Beliefs
82 The Power of Persistence

86 **Defining Your Purpose: Giving Meaning to Your Life**
    Exploring Different Approaches to Defining Purpose
91 Connecting Purpose to Values and Passions
95 Purpose as a Guiding Star
100 Purpose in Action: Practical Application
104 The Evolving Nature of Purpose

110   **Life of Purpose: Actionable Strategies**
      Setting Meaningful Goals
114   Supportive Environment
119   Managing Challenges and Setbacks
123   Celebrating Milestones and Progress
127   Continues Growth and Self-reflection

132   **Embracing Your Authentic Self**
      The Power of Self-Acceptance
137   Self-Compassion
142   Building Healthy Connections
147   Contributing to Something Larger than Yourself
151   Fulfillment
      A Final Reflection

157   **The Alchemist Within**

161   **Sculpting the Masterpiece of Self**

This book is dedicated to the countless individuals who have embarked on their own journeys of self-discovery, bravely facing their inner demons and emerging stronger, wiser, and more authentic. It is dedicated to those who have dared to question societal norms, to challenge their own limiting beliefs, and to embrace the messy, beautiful process of becoming their truest selves. This is for the dreamers, the doubters, the warriors, and the quiet souls who carry a universe within. It is a confirmation of the resilience of the human spirit, the infinite capacity for growth, and the unwavering power of self-belief. It is also dedicated to the unwavering support of my family and friends, whose love and encouragement fueled my own journey and continues to inspire me to share this message of hope and transformation with the world. Their belief in me, even when I doubted myself, gave me the strength to overcome obstacles and find the courage to share my story.

This book is a product of their steadfast faith and unconditional love, a gift to them as much as it is to the reader. This journey of self-discovery is not a solitary endeavor; it thrives on connection and shared experiences, strengthened by the unwavering presence of those who believe in our potential.

May this book serve as a reminder of the power of human connection and the importance of celebrating each other's victories along the path to personal growth and fulfillment. To you, I dedicate this heartfelt expression of gratitude and inspiration.

PREFACE

For many years, I lived a life that felt…off. Externally, I had it all: a successful career, a loving family, a comfortable life. Yet, internally, I felt a deep sense of unease, a persistent whisper of dissatisfaction. I chased achievements, accolades, and external validation, believing that these things would somehow fill the void within. They didn't. In fact, they amplified the emptiness. My journey to finding my true self wasn't a straightforward, linear path. It was a winding road, fraught with moments of self-doubt, fear, and uncertainty. It involved confronting deeply ingrained beliefs, confronting painful memories, and letting go of the narratives I had created around my identity. It required embracing vulnerability, acknowledging my imperfections, and accepting the fact that I wasn't always in control.

This book is a culmination of that journey, a distillation of the lessons learned, the challenges overcome, and the profound sense of peace and fulfillment I've finally found. It's not a quick-fix guide, nor does it offer easy answers to life's complexities. Instead, it's an invitation to embark on your own unique journey of self-discovery — a journey that will require courage, honesty, and a willingness to confront the uncomfortable truths that lie within.

Through personal anecdotes, introspective exercises, and a compassionate approach, I hope to guide you toward a deeper understanding of yourself, your values, and your purpose. It's my sincere hope that this book will empower you to shed the masks you wear, embrace your authentic self, and create a life that truly resonates with your soul. This is not a journey for the faint of heart, but I can assure you, the rewards are worth every ounce of effort. Be brave, be vulnerable, and most importantly, be true to yourself.

INTRODUCTION

Are you feeling lost, unfulfilled, or disconnected from your true self? Do you find yourself chasing external validation, seeking approval from others instead of honoring your own inner compass? If so, you are not alone. Many individuals, despite achieving external success, grapple with a persistent sense of emptiness, a nagging feeling that something is missing. This book, "The Alchemy of Self-Discovery," is a guide to help you navigate the complexities of self-discovery, to unearth your authentic self, and to create a life that aligns with your deepest values and aspirations. We will explore the societal pressures that often shape our sense of self, creating a disconnect between our external lives and our inner desires. We'll delve into the importance of self-reflection, identifying your core values, uncovering hidden passions, and defining a purpose that resonates deeply within you.

 This isn't simply about identifying your strengths; it's about embracing your vulnerabilities, acknowledging your imperfections, and celebrating the unique fabric of your being. This book offers a practical framework for personal growth, incorporating introspective prompts, journaling exercises, and real-world examples to guide your journey. It's a call to action, an invitation to shed the masks you wear, confront your fears, and step into the radiant light of your authentic self. Prepare for a transformative experience. Prepare to discover the incredible person you were always meant to be.

This journey may be challenging, requiring introspection and courage. Yet, the reward of living a life aligned with your true self is immeasurable.

THE UNCOMFORTABLE TRUTH

CONFRONTING THE GAP BETWEEN EXPECTATION AND REALITY

UNMASKING SOCIETAL EXPECTATIONS

We live in a world saturated with expectations. From the moment we're born, a labyrinth of societal norms, family traditions, and cultural beliefs begins to weave itself around us, shaping our understanding of who we *should* be. These aren't necessarily malicious impositions; often, they're well-intentioned suggestions, passed down through generations or absorbed from the media, friends, and family. But the insidious nature of these expectations lies in their capacity to subtly, and sometimes not-so-subtly, suffocate our authentic selves. We begin to mold ourselves to fit pre-defined molds, sacrificing our individual desires and aspirations on the altar of conformity.

Think about the pressure to achieve academic excellence, often fueled by the desire to meet parental expectations or secure a prestigious career. The relentless pursuit of material success, fueled by societal messages equating wealth with happiness and fulfillment, can leave us feeling hollow even when we reach our financial goals. The idealized images of relationships portrayed in movies and television can create unrealistic expectations about love and partnership, leaving us feeling inadequate or perpetually searching for something unattainable. The pressure to conform to specific beauty standards, perpetuated by advertising and social media, can lead to body image issues and a constant struggle for self-acceptance.

These pressures are not confined to specific demographics or socioeconomic groups. They transcend age, gender, race, and cultural background. The expectation to achieve a certain level of professional success can weigh heavily on a young entrepreneur just starting their business, a mid-career professional feeling stalled, or even a retiree who feels pressured to remain active and productive. Similarly, the expectation to maintain a picture-perfect family life can impact parents across diverse socio-economic strata, leading to immense pressure and feelings of inadequacy. The pressure to maintain a certain social image, carefully curated for social media consumption, knows no bounds, affecting everyone from teenagers to adults navigating the complexities of online interactions.

The impact of these pervasive societal expectations is far-reaching. It often leads to the creation of a false self, a carefully constructed persona designed to meet the demands of others while suppressing our true desires and vulnerabilities. This disconnect between our outward presentation and our inner world creates a deep sense of dissonance, manifesting as feelings of inadequacy, anxiety, depression, and a pervasive sense of unfulfillment. We become masters of disguise, adept at playing roles that don't truly reflect who we are.

This false self can manifest in various ways. We may suppress our true feelings and opinions to avoid conflict or disapproval, sacrificing our authenticity for the sake of social harmony. We might pursue careers that offer security and stability but hold little intrinsic interest, prioritizing the expectations of others over our own passions. We may engage in relationships that lack genuine connection, settling for something less than fulfilling to avoid the perceived risk of loneliness or rejection.

The consequences of this self-betrayal are profound. The constant effort to maintain this facade can lead to chronic stress, burnout, and feelings of emptiness. We may find ourselves constantly comparing ourselves to others, fueling feelings of inadequacy and envy. Our relationships may become strained, as we struggle to connect with others authentically while simultaneously maintaining our carefully constructed personas. We might find ourselves feeling lost and directionless, unsure of our true values and aspirations.

Consider the individual who, pressured to follow a traditional career path by their family, becomes a successful lawyer despite harboring a deep passion for art. They may achieve external validation, earning respect and financial security. But inwardly, they might experience a gnawing sense of unfulfillment, a constant reminder of the dreams sacrificed at the altar of expectation. The weight of their unlived life can lead to chronic stress, anxiety, and a persistent sense of dissatisfaction. Their success becomes a hollow victory, overshadowed by the quiet ache of an unfulfilled life.

Or consider the woman who, despite her independent spirit, conforms to societal expectations of marriage and motherhood, suppressing her desire for a career in a competitive field. She may create a seemingly perfect family life, but internally she battles feelings of frustration and resentment, a silent scream of unfulfilled potential. This internal conflict can strain her relationships, leading to misunderstandings and resentment. Her sense of self-worth may become intricately tied to her external roles, creating a dependency that leaves her feeling vulnerable and unfulfilled.

These are not isolated cases. They represent a widespread experience of navigating the complex terrain of societal expectations and personal aspirations. The crucial first step towards reclaiming our authentic selves involves recognizing the pervasive influence of these expectations and acknowledging the gap between our outward presentation and our inner desires. It is a journey of self-discovery that requires courage, honesty, and a willingness to confront uncomfortable truths about ourselves and the world we inhabit. This is not about rejecting societal norms entirely, but about discerning which expectations serve us and which ones hinder our growth. It's about reclaiming our agency and making conscious choices that align with our deepest values and aspirations. The journey of finding our true selves begins with acknowledging the influence of external pressures and their impact on our sense of self. Only then can we begin to dismantle the carefully constructed facades and uncover the authentic selves that lie beneath.

The next step in this journey involves a deep dive into the internal conflicts that arise from this dissonance. The struggle between ambition and fear, the tension between conformity and self-expression – these are common internal battles that fuel the feeling of being out of sync with ourselves. We often find ourselves caught in a tug-of-war between what we believe we *should* do and what we truly *want* to do.

Understanding the roots of these conflicts, acknowledging the validity of both sides, and developing strategies to navigate them is crucial in this process of self-discovery. This involves facing our fears head-on, challenging our limiting beliefs, and accepting the fact that it's okay to be imperfect. Perfection is an illusion; authenticity is a journey, not a destination.

Many individuals experience the internal conflict between their creative passions and the practical demands of life. They may dream of writing a novel, starting a business, or pursuing a creative art form, but societal pressures dictate the pursuit of stable employment and financial security. This internal tug-of-war can lead to feelings of guilt, frustration, and a constant sense of being "behind" in life's race. Others may face the internal conflict between personal ambition and the desire for connection and intimacy. They might crave professional success, but fear that pursuing their ambitious goals will compromise their relationships or lead to loneliness. This struggle highlights the complex interplay between our individual aspirations and our deep-seated need for belonging and connection.

Yet another internal conflict arises from the tension between conforming to societal expectations and expressing one's true self. Individuals may feel immense pressure to fit in, to adhere to established norms and expectations, while simultaneously harboring a deep desire to express their unique individuality. This conflict can manifest as feelings of anxiety, self-doubt, and a fear of judgment. They may censor their thoughts and feelings, afraid of being ostracized or rejected for their authenticity. This constant suppression of individuality takes a toll on their mental and emotional well-being. The fear of non-conformity often stems from a deep-seated insecurity or a need for external validation, making it crucial to address these underlying anxieties.

The journey towards authenticity involves recognizing these internal conflicts and developing strategies to manage them effectively. This requires self-awareness, honesty, and a willingness to confront the complexities of our inner landscape. It's about finding a balance between our individual desires and the responsibilities we have towards others. It's about accepting that it's okay to make mistakes, to change our minds, and to evolve over time. There is no single path to self-discovery; the journey is unique to each individual.

Recognizing the symptoms of this disconnect between our external lives and internal desires is vital. Feeling empty despite outward success, experiencing chronic anxiety or depression despite having a seemingly perfect life, or lacking a sense of purpose or meaning are all telltale signs that something is amiss. These feelings are not simply a matter of being "negative" or "whiny"—they are valid indicators that we are living out of alignment with our true selves. They are a cry for authenticity, a desperate plea to return to the path of our true being.

These symptoms are not always dramatic or easily identifiable. They can manifest as subtle feelings of discontent, a persistent sense of restlessness, or a nagging feeling that something is missing. These feelings are often dismissed as temporary or insignificant, yet they can be a persistent source of dissatisfaction and unhappiness. Chronic fatigue, difficulty sleeping, difficulty concentrating, a lack of joy in everyday activities, and feeling trapped or helpless are also potential symptoms of this internal disconnect. The key is to pay attention to our inner landscape, to notice the subtle cues that our bodies and minds are sending us, and to address these issues before they escalate into something larger. The path to our authentic selves requires that we become mindful and observant.

The first step towards healing lies in confronting these difficult feelings, acknowledging their validity, and refusing to ignore the messages our bodies and minds are sending us. By acknowledging our internal struggles, we can begin the process of healing and transformation. This involves creating space for self-reflection, confronting our fears, and accepting our imperfections. It is a process that requires patience, courage, and self-compassion. There is no shortcut to self-discovery; it is a lifelong journey that requires continuous effort and commitment.

IDENTIFYING YOUR INTERNAL CONFLICTS

The discomfort of confronting the gap between expectation and reality often stems from internal conflicts that simmer beneath the surface of our daily lives. These aren't simple disagreements; they are deeply ingrained battles between opposing forces within ourselves, often rooted in conflicting values, desires, and fears. Understanding these internal struggles is crucial to bridge the gap between who we are and who we aspire to be.

One of the most prevalent internal conflicts is the tug-of-war between ambition and fear. We are often told to dream big, to chase our aspirations with unwavering determination. Society champions the go-getter, the entrepreneur, the individual who relentlessly pursues their goals. Yet, simultaneously, a powerful counterforce—fear—whispers doubts and anxieties into our ears. Fear of failure, fear of judgment, fear of the unknown can paralyze us, preventing us from even taking the first step towards our dreams. This internal conflict can manifest in procrastination, self-sabotage, and a constant state of anxiety.

I remember wrestling with this conflict myself. For years, I harbored a deep desire to write again, to share my experiences and insights with the world. The ambition burned brightly within me, fueled by a passion to connect with others on a deeper level. But the fear was equally potent. Fear of rejection, of criticism, of pouring my heart and soul into a project only to have it fall flat. The fear whispered insidious doubts: *What if nobody reads it? What if it's terrible? What if I'm not good enough?* These anxieties held me back for years, creating a frustrating cycle of starting and abandoning projects, never allowing myself to fully commit to my ambition. It wasn't until I consciously acknowledged the fear, and validated its presence without letting it dictate my actions, that I was finally able to move forward. I began by writing small pieces, sharing them with trusted friends for feedback, and gradually building my confidence. It wasn't a linear path; there were setbacks and moments of self-doubt, but the acknowledgment of the internal conflict allowed me to navigate these challenges with greater self-awareness.

Another pervasive internal conflict arises from the tension between conformity and authenticity. We live in a society that often rewards conformity. Fitting in, adhering to established norms, and following the expected path can lead to a sense of security and acceptance. But at what cost? Suppressing our unique identities, our individual passions, and our dissenting viewpoints can lead to a profound sense of emptiness and dissatisfaction. The conflict arises from the inherent desire to belong, to be accepted, versus the equally powerful urge to express our true selves, even if it means standing apart from the crowd.

Many of us face this internal struggle. We might outwardly conform to societal expectations—choosing a career path our family approves of, adhering to certain social norms, or suppressing our individuality—while inwardly yearning for something more, something truer to our own unique selves. This internal dissonance can manifest as feelings of resentment, frustration, or a nagging sense of unfulfillment. We might find ourselves constantly comparing ourselves to others, feeling inadequate or envious of those who appear to have it all figured out. But true fulfillment rarely comes from mimicking others; it stems from embracing our own authentic selves, even when it means deviating from the prescribed path.

I've witnessed this conflict play out countless times. One friend, a successful lawyer, confided in me about her deep-seated unhappiness despite her outwardly impressive achievements. She'd always felt pressured to pursue a legal career, fulfilling her family's expectations of professional success. But her heart belonged to the arts. The internal conflict between conforming to external pressures and expressing her true artistic passion caused significant anxiety and dissatisfaction. By confronting this conflict, acknowledging the validity of her artistic desires and the societal pressures she faced, she was able to begin making changes, eventually transitioning into a career that combined her legal skills with her artistic passions. It wasn't an easy transition, but it was a deeply transformative one.

Another common internal conflict is the battle between self-criticism and self-compassion. Many of us are our own harshest critics, constantly judging our flaws, shortcomings, and perceived inadequacies. We replay our mistakes in our minds, dwelling on our imperfections and minimizing our successes. This relentless self-criticism can lead to low self-esteem, anxiety, and depression. However, the path to healing and self-acceptance involves cultivating self-compassion — treating ourselves with the same kindness, understanding, and forgiveness that we would offer a close friend.

Our self-critical voice, the one that constantly points out flaws and failures, is often deeply rooted in past experiences, insecurities, or learned behavior. It's not necessarily accurate or helpful.

Learning to differentiate between constructive criticism and self-destructive negativity is a key step. Developing self-compassion involves acknowledging our imperfections without judging ourselves harshly. It's about recognizing that we are all flawed, imperfect beings and that making mistakes is part of the human experience. It involves practicing self-forgiveness, letting go of past regrets, and focusing on self-growth rather than self-reproach.

The conflict between immediate gratification and long-term goals is another significant internal struggle. Our modern society is often structured around immediate rewards — instant access to information, instant shopping experiences, and immediate emotional gratification through social media. This can make it challenging to prioritize long-term goals that require sustained effort, delayed gratification, and consistent commitment. The internal conflict arises from the pull between our desire for immediate pleasure and our aspiration for a more fulfilling and meaningful future.

I've seen this conflict manifest in many ways, from procrastination on important tasks to impulsive spending habits. The key is to cultivate mindful awareness of these impulses. By recognizing the pattern of choosing immediate gratification over long-term goals, we can begin to make conscious choices to prioritize our future selves. This involves setting realistic goals, breaking down large tasks into smaller, manageable steps, and developing strategies for delaying gratification. It's about recognizing the importance of building a strong foundation for the future, even when it requires sacrifices in the present.

The internal conflict between independence and connection is a deeply human struggle. We all have an inherent need for autonomy and self-reliance, for charting our own course and defining our own path. Simultaneously, we crave connection, belonging, and meaningful relationships. The tension arises from the need to maintain our individuality while also forging strong bonds with others. Too much independence can lead to isolation and loneliness, while too much dependence can stifle our personal growth and autonomy.

This conflict is often subtly present in our relationships. We might find ourselves constantly navigating the balance between maintaining our individual identity and fulfilling our responsibilities within a relationship. It's a dance between self-expression and compromise, between setting boundaries and maintaining intimacy. Understanding this delicate balance is crucial to fostering healthy and fulfilling relationships, and it demands an ongoing dialogue with ourselves about our needs and boundaries.

Identifying these internal conflicts isn't about assigning blame or judging ourselves harshly. Instead, it's about gaining a deeper understanding of the forces at play within us, the internal dialogues and subconscious motivations that shape our choices and actions. It's about acknowledging the complexities of the human experience and recognizing that these conflicts are normal, even inevitable. By bringing these internal battles into the light, we create space for self-awareness, self-acceptance, and ultimately, self-transformation. The journey of self-discovery involves confronting these challenges head-on, learning to navigate them with grace, and embracing the messy, imperfect beauty of being human. This process of understanding and integrating these diverse aspects of ourselves is what ultimately bridges the gap between expectation and reality, leading us closer to a life aligned with our truest selves.

RECOGNIZING THE SYMPTOMS OF DISCONNECTION

The chasm between expectation and reality isn't a sudden, dramatic crack; it's more like a slow, insidious erosion, subtly chipping away at our sense of self until we're left feeling adrift, disconnected from the life we thought we wanted. Recognizing the symptoms of this disconnect is the first, crucial step towards bridging the gap. It's about acknowledging the subtle whispers of discontent that often masquerade as everyday frustrations, before they escalate into full-blown crises.

One of the most pervasive symptoms is a persistent feeling of emptiness, a hollowness that no amount of external achievement can fill. This isn't simply sadness or a temporary slump; it's a deeper, more profound sense of lacking something essential, a fundamental void at the core of one's being. Imagine a successful lawyer, lauded for their sharp intellect and impressive career trajectory, yet feeling utterly unfulfilled, their evenings spent staring blankly at the television, a profound sense of disconnect separating them from their accomplishments.

The outward success doesn't translate to inner peace or contentment. This is a stark indicator that something is amiss, that the external narrative of their life doesn't align with their inner truth.

This emptiness often manifests as a pervasive sense of anxiety, a low-level hum of unease that permeates daily life. This anxiety isn't necessarily tied to specific events or problems; rather, it's a general feeling of unease, a subtle dread that something is fundamentally wrong. This could present as difficulty concentrating, insomnia, or an increased susceptibility to stress. Consider a stay-at-home mother, seemingly living the idyllic life – a beautiful home, a loving family, yet perpetually anxious. She feels trapped, her days blurring into a monotonous routine that suffocates her spirit, despite outwardly appearing content to the casual observer. This persistent anxiety is a signal that her inner world is crying out for attention, a stark reminder that the externally fulfilling life she portrays doesn't reflect her internal state.

Another significant symptom is a profound lack of purpose. This isn't merely a lack of ambition; it's a deeper sense of meaninglessness, a feeling that life lacks direction or significance. Individuals struggling with this disconnect often find themselves adrift, lacking a sense of purpose or fulfillment in their work, relationships, or daily activities. They may feel like they are merely going through the motions, participating in a life that feels detached from their true self. Picture a talented artist, working a mundane corporate job to pay the bills, their creative passions stifled and ignored. Each day feels like a slow erosion of their spirit, a gradual diminishing of their inner light. The lack of purpose, the absence of aligning their actions with their deepest values, creates a constant internal conflict, leading to this profound sense of disconnect.

This feeling of being out of sync can also manifest as a chronic dissatisfaction with life, a persistent sense of discontent that permeates various aspects of one's life. This isn't simply mild unhappiness; it's a deep-seated dissatisfaction with the direction of one's life, relationships, or career. This dissatisfaction isn't easily alleviated by minor changes; it's a fundamental feeling that something is significantly wrong, that the current path isn't leading to a fulfilling destination. A successful entrepreneur, surrounded by wealth and accolades, might constantly feel dissatisfied.

The relentless pursuit of external validation leaves us emotionally empty, despite our outwardly impressive achievements.

This demonstrates a fundamental disconnect between their external life and their internal desires, showcasing how external success doesn't always equate to inner fulfillment.

Beyond these prominent symptoms, there are subtler signs that often indicate a growing disconnect. These can include a persistent feeling of being misunderstood, a sense that no one truly "gets" you. This can lead to isolation and loneliness, even when surrounded by people. This feeling isn't merely about a lack of communication; it's a deeper sense of being unseen, unheard, your true self remaining hidden beneath a carefully constructed façade. Think of a highly social individual, always surrounded by friends, yet feeling profoundly lonely.

Their social connections offer only superficial interaction, lacking the genuine connection that they yearn for. This demonstrates how a full social life can exist alongside a profound feeling of inner isolation and disconnect.

Another subtle indicator is a lack of passion or enthusiasm for activities you once enjoyed. This gradual waning of interest can manifest as apathy towards hobbies, relationships, or even life itself. This is more than just boredom; it's a symptom of a soul searching for something more authentic, something deeply resonant with its true nature. For example, a passionate musician who suddenly finds playing their instrument a chore, their once-vibrant melodies replaced by a sense of drudgery, is experiencing this silent scream from their soul. This fading passion points towards a disconnect between their present actions and their deeper, more soulful aspirations.

Furthermore, a persistent feeling of being "stuck" is a critical symptom of this inner divide. This isn't merely a temporary setback;

it's a pervasive feeling of being trapped in a life that no longer resonates with your authentic self. This might manifest as a reluctance to try new things, a feeling of inertia that prevents positive change. Imagine a person feeling trapped in a dead-end job, feeling utterly powerless to make changes. This inability to navigate towards a more fulfilling path indicates a deep-seated disconnect between their aspiration and their perceived reality.

Physical symptoms can also be strong indicators of this inner turmoil. Chronic fatigue, unexplained aches and pains, and digestive problems can all be manifestations of unresolved inner conflicts. The body, after all, is a reflection of the mind and spirit. Ignoring these physical manifestations is like ignoring the warning lights on a dashboard – it ultimately leads to more significant problems down the road. For example, a person experiencing constant headaches and digestive issues, despite regular checkups and good health, could be experiencing the physical manifestation of their disconnect. These physical symptoms serve as a powerful reminder that emotional well-being is directly connected to physical well-being.

A significant shift in values or beliefs can also signal a growing disconnect. This isn't simply a change of opinion; it's a fundamental realignment of one's core principles, often driven by an unconscious desire for greater authenticity.

It's a recognition that the values you once held no longer align with your current understanding of yourself. For instance, an individual who once prioritized career success above all else, suddenly finding themselves prioritizing family and personal well-being, is undergoing a significant internal shift. This internal re-evaluation showcases the inherent drive towards greater alignment between the external life and internal values.

Recognizing these symptoms isn't about self-criticism; it's about self-compassion. It's about acknowledging that this disconnect is a common human experience, a natural byproduct of living in a world that often pressures us to conform to unrealistic expectations. The crucial step is acknowledging the dissonance, opening ourselves to the possibility that there's a gap between who we are and who we believe we should be. This awareness is the cornerstone of bridging the gap, the starting point of a journey towards greater self-understanding and ultimately, a more authentic and fulfilling life. The path ahead may be challenging, but it's a journey well worth undertaking. It's a journey of rediscovering your true self, and reclaiming the life that's rightfully yours.

The alchemy of self-discovery is found in the boundless expanse of your soul's sea. Allow its currents to carry you beyond familiar shores, and you will discover the treasures hidden in your depths.

UNVEILING YOUR INNER WORLD

The discomfort of acknowledging the gap between expectation and reality can feel overwhelming. It's a feeling many of us share, a silent struggle played out in the quiet moments of our lives. But the path towards bridging that gap isn't paved with quick fixes or easy answers. It's a journey inward, a voyage of self-discovery that begins with a single, crucial step: self-reflection.

Self-reflection isn't some esoteric practice reserved for monks in mountaintop monasteries; it's a practical, powerful tool available to each and every one of us. It's about turning the lens of our awareness inward, examining our thoughts, feelings, and behaviors with a gentle curiosity, not harsh judgment. Think of it as a conversation with your inner self, a dialogue aimed at uncovering the hidden narratives shaping your perceptions and actions.

This process might feel daunting initially. Many of us are accustomed to a constant outward focus, a whirlwind of activity that keeps us from pausing to truly examine our internal landscape. We're so busy striving for external validation, chasing elusive goals dictated by societal pressures or inherited expectations, that we rarely carve out time for introspection. This constant external focus prevents us from truly understanding our own inner world. But just as a ship needs a compass to navigate uncharted waters, we need self-reflection to navigate the complexities of our own lives.

One of the most accessible tools for self-reflection is journaling. It's a simple yet profound practice that allows us to externalize our thoughts and feelings, giving them form and clarity. Instead of letting them swirl around in our minds, creating a muddled sense of unease, we can put them down on paper, allowing for examination and understanding. Start with simple prompts, such as:

"What are my biggest sources of stress right now?"

"What are my deepest fears and insecurities?"

"What brings me genuine joy and fulfillment?"

"What are my core values, and am I living in accordance with them?"

"Where do I feel a disconnect between who I am and who I want to be?"

"What is one small step I can take towards bridging that gap?"

Don't worry about crafting perfectly polished prose. The goal isn't literary excellence; it's honest self-expression. Let your thoughts flow freely, without editing or censoring. Allow yourself to be vulnerable, to explore the darker corners of your psyche as well as the sunlit meadows. The act of writing itself can be incredibly therapeutic, offering a safe space for processing emotions and identifying patterns of thought and behavior.

Guided meditation offers another powerful avenue for self-reflection. Meditation allows us to quiet the incessant chatter of the mind, creating a space for observing our thoughts and feelings without judgment. Numerous guided meditations are available online, often focusing on self-compassion, mindfulness, and emotional regulation. These guided exercises can help us to develop the capacity to observe our inner world with greater clarity and understanding. Even five to ten minutes of daily meditation can make a significant difference in our ability to connect with our inner selves.

SELF-REFLECTION ISN'T ABOUT SELF-CRITICISM.

It's not about finding fault or dwelling on our shortcomings. Rather, it's about fostering self-compassion and understanding. It's about acknowledging our imperfections, accepting our vulnerabilities, and recognizing the inherent worthiness within ourselves. It's about cultivating a sense of self-acceptance, embracing the full spectrum of our emotions—the joy and sorrow, the triumphs and setbacks—as integral parts of the human experience.

Consider this scenario: Imagine you've always dreamed of being a writer, pouring your heart and soul into crafting compelling stories. You envisioned yourself as a successful novelist, celebrated for your unique voice and insightful prose. Yet, years have passed, and you're still working a job you dislike, your dreams relegated to the dusty corners of your mind. The gap between expectation and reality is vast, leaving you feeling disillusioned and unfulfilled.

Self-reflection, in this case, would involve exploring the underlying reasons for this disconnect. Perhaps fear of failure has held you back. Perhaps self-doubt has whispered insidious lies, convincing you that your writing isn't good enough. Perhaps the societal pressures to pursue a more "stable" career path have overridden your creative aspirations. By examining these internal narratives, you begin to dismantle the barriers that have kept you from pursuing your passion.

Self-reflection might reveal that you actually possess immense talent but lack the confidence to showcase it. It could highlight the need for setting achievable goals, starting with small steps, rather than aiming for immediate grand success. Perhaps it would bring to light the necessity to overcome the fear of judgment from others. Through this process, you might discover that the "gap" isn't insurmountable, but rather a series of obstacles that can be overcome with conscious effort and self-belief.

The alchemy of self-discovery lies in turning the lead of your limitations into the pure, shining spirit of your potential.

Let's delve into another example. Imagine you've always strived for perfectionism in your career. You've pushed yourself relentlessly, sacrificing personal relationships and well-being in the pursuit of excellence. The result? Burnout and a deep sense of emptiness. The gap here lies between the relentless striving for external validation and the neglect of your own emotional and physical needs.

Through self-reflection, you might realize that your relentless pursuit of perfection stems from a deep-seated insecurity, a fear of not being good enough. This self-examination might lead you to question the very definition of success. Perhaps success isn't solely defined by external achievements, but also by inner peace, healthy relationships, and a sense of balance in your life. Through this understanding, you can begin to redefine your values and priorities, prioritizing self-care and mindful living alongside professional aspirations.

Self-reflection is not a one-time event; it's an ongoing process, a lifelong journey of self-discovery. It requires patience, perseverance, and a commitment to honesty with yourself. There will be times when the insights gained are uncomfortable, even painful. But facing these uncomfortable truths is essential for personal growth and transformation. It's in these moments of vulnerability that we find the strength and resilience to bridge the gap between expectation and reality.

Consider setting aside dedicated time each week for self-reflection. This could be a quiet evening with a journal and a cup of tea, or a morning meditation session before the day begins. Create a sacred space where you can disconnect from the external world and reconnect with your inner self. Don't rush the process. Allow yourself ample time to explore your thoughts and feelings, without judgment or self-criticism.

Embrace the power of questions. Ask yourself probing questions about your relationships, your career, your values, your goals, and your overall sense of well-being. Don't be afraid to delve deep, to explore the uncomfortable aspects of your life as well as the positive ones. The more honest you are with yourself, the greater the clarity and understanding you'll achieve.

Remember, the journey of self-discovery is personal and unique. There is no right or wrong way to reflect; the key is to find a method that resonates with you and allows you to connect with your inner self. Whether it's through journaling, meditation, nature walks, spending time in solitude, or engaging in creative pursuits, the important thing is to create space for introspection and exploration. The insights gained will be invaluable, guiding you on a path toward a more authentic and fulfilling life. And remember, the process itself is as important as the outcome. The act of self-reflection demonstrates your commitment to your personal growth and to uncovering the magnificent individual you truly are. Embrace the journey, and trust the process. The rewards of self-understanding are immeasurable.

EMBRACING VULNERABILITY: A PATH TO AUTHENTICITY

The journey towards bridging the gap between expectation and reality isn't solely about introspection; it's about action, about daring to step outside the carefully constructed walls of our perceived selves. This requires embracing vulnerability, a concept often misunderstood and feared. We've been conditioned to equate vulnerability with weakness, with a lack of control. But vulnerability, in its truest form, is the courageous act of showing up authentically, imperfections and all. It's the willingness to be seen, truly seen, with all our flaws and insecurities laid bare.

This isn't about seeking pity or validation; it's about liberating ourselves from the burden of constantly trying to project an image of perfection. The irony is that this relentless pursuit of flawlessness often leaves us feeling more isolated and disconnected than ever. We build walls around ourselves, protecting our perceived vulnerabilities, but in doing so, we also shut out opportunities for genuine connection and profound self-understanding.

Embrace vulnerability as a sacred act of self-acceptance. It is in those tender spaces that we find our resilience and our capacity for love.

Think about a time you felt deeply connected to someone. Was it when you were both meticulously crafting perfect facades, engaging in small talk and avoiding anything remotely personal? Or was it when a moment of shared vulnerability occurred — a confession, a shared struggle, a moment of raw honesty? The power of connection lies in shared vulnerability. It fosters trust, intimacy, and a sense of belonging. It allows us to see that we're not alone in our struggles, that our imperfections are not unique, and that our vulnerabilities are, in fact, what make us human.

Embracing vulnerability doesn't mean throwing caution to the wind and revealing every detail of our lives to everyone we meet. It's a nuanced process, a gradual unveiling of our true selves to those who have earned our trust.

It begins with small steps — sharing a personal struggle with a close friend, expressing a difficult emotion, and admitting a mistake. Each act of vulnerability, however small, strengthens our capacity for deeper connection and self-acceptance.

Many of us have been raised with the belief that vulnerability equates to weakness. We've learned to suppress our emotions, hide our imperfections, and maintain a polished exterior. But this carefully constructed image often comes at a significant cost. It leaves us feeling exhausted, isolated, and disconnected from ourselves and others. It prevents us from forming authentic relationships, pursuing our passions, and living a life aligned with our values.

Consider the impact of social media on our perception of vulnerability. We are constantly bombarded with curated images of seemingly perfect lives, leading many to believe that vulnerability is a sign of failure. This creates a climate where authenticity is stifled, replaced by a relentless pursuit of an unattainable ideal. This only exacerbates the inherent discomfort we already feel when contemplating showing our true selves.

Breaking free from this cycle requires a conscious effort to challenge these ingrained beliefs. It demands that we redefine vulnerability not as weakness but as strength. It takes courage to be vulnerable, to expose ourselves to the possibility of judgment or rejection. But the rewards far outweigh the risks. By embracing our vulnerabilities, we open ourselves up to authentic connections, deeper self-understanding, and a more fulfilling life.

One of the most transformative aspects of embracing vulnerability is the acceptance of our imperfections. We are not meant to be perfect; our imperfections are what make us unique, interesting, and relatable. They are part of our story, shaping our experiences and contributing to our growth. Yet, society often pressures us to hide these imperfections, to strive for an unrealistic standard of perfection. This relentless pursuit of perfection only serves to heighten our self-criticism and fuel our insecurities.

The path to self-acceptance begins with recognizing and accepting our imperfections. This isn't about self-indulgence or complacency; it's about cultivating self-compassion. It's about treating ourselves with the same kindness and understanding we would offer a close friend struggling with similar challenges. It requires that we challenge our negative self-talk, replacing self-criticism with self-encouragement. We need to learn to embrace our flaws as integral parts of our unique identity, recognizing that they don't diminish our worth.

Self-acceptance is the quiet revolution within, the gentle acknowledgment that you are worthy, exactly as you are, in this very moment.

Take some time each day to write about your thoughts and feelings, including your insecurities and imperfections. Allow yourself to explore your vulnerabilities without judgment. Observe your patterns of self-criticism and try to reframe your negative thoughts into more positive and compassionate ones. Over time, this practice will foster a deeper understanding of yourself and help you cultivate self-compassion.

Another helpful strategy is to engage in self-reflection exercises focused on identifying and challenging your negative beliefs. Ask yourself: What are my core beliefs about myself? Are these beliefs accurate and helpful? Where do these beliefs originate? By understanding the roots of our self-criticism, we can begin to challenge and dismantle those negative beliefs that hold us back.

REMEMBER, EMBRACING VULNERABILITY IS A CONTINUOUS PROCESS OF GROWTH AND SELF-DISCOVERY.

There will be times when we stumble, when we feel exposed and vulnerable. But these moments are opportunities for learning and growth. They are opportunities to practice self-compassion and to develop greater resilience. It's in these moments of vulnerability that we truly connect with ourselves and others, forging stronger relationships and a deeper sense of self-acceptance.

Embracing vulnerability allows us to develop greater empathy and compassion for others. When we are willing to share our own vulnerabilities, we create a space for others to do the same. This fosters a sense of connection and belonging, allowing us to see that we are not alone in our struggles. It creates a supportive environment where people feel safe to be themselves, imperfections and all.

Vulnerability is not about exposing your wounds, but about revealing your heart.
The most profound transformations arise from the courage to be vulnerable. It is in those raw, honest moments that we find our shared humanity and build bridges of understanding.

Consider the power of storytelling in this context. Sharing our vulnerabilities through stories allows us to connect with others on a deeper level, forging bonds based on shared experiences. These stories don't have to be grand narratives; they can be simple accounts of everyday struggles and triumphs. By sharing our stories, we not only help ourselves but also inspire and support others on their journey of self-discovery.

Embracing vulnerability can lead to unexpected opportunities for personal and professional growth. When we are willing to step outside our comfort zones and show our true selves, we often discover hidden talents, strengths, and passions. This increased self-awareness can lead to new career paths, more fulfilling relationships, and a greater sense of purpose in life.

The journey to embrace vulnerability is not always easy. It requires courage, self-compassion, and a willingness to be seen for who we truly are. However, the rewards are immeasurable. By shedding the masks we wear and embracing our authentic selves, we open ourselves up to deeper connections, greater self-acceptance, and a more fulfilling life. It's a path towards living a life aligned with our true values and aspirations, a life free from the constraints of societal expectations and the burden of trying to be someone we are not. It's a path to finding the beautiful, imperfect, and ultimately authentic you. And that, my friends, is a journey worth taking.

Vulnerability is the key to authenticity. By embracing our imperfections and sharing our true selves, we build deeper and more meaningful connections with others.

UNDERSTANDING YOUR VALUES
THE COMPASS OF YOUR SOUL

IDENTIFYING CORE VALUES

Our journey of self-discovery continues, and in this chapter, we delve into a crucial element of understanding who we truly are: our core values. These aren't just fleeting preferences; they're the deeply held beliefs that guide our decisions, shape our behaviors, and ultimately define our sense of self. Identifying these values is akin to finding the compass needle within our souls, pointing us towards a life of authenticity and purpose.

Think of your values as the foundation upon which your life is built. A house without a solid foundation is unstable, prone to collapse under pressure. Similarly, a life built without a clear understanding of your core values can feel directionless, leading to dissatisfaction and a sense of being adrift.

So, how do we unearth these deeply ingrained beliefs? It's not always a simple task. Our values often lie buried beneath layers of societal expectations, learned behaviors, and perhaps even self-deception. It requires introspection, honest self-reflection, and a willingness to confront uncomfortable truths about ourselves. But the reward – a life lived in alignment with your true self – is immeasurable.

ONE POWERFUL TECHNIQUE IS TO CONSIDER THE MOMENTS IN YOUR LIFE WHEN YOU FELT MOST ALIVE, MOST FULFILLED.

QUESTION YOURSELF: What were you doing?

Who were you with?

What were the circumstances?

Analyze these memories; they hold valuable clues. Look for recurring themes, patterns, and emotions.

- Did you feel a sense of purpose, connection, or accomplishment?
- Were you contributing to something larger than yourself?
- These feelings often point directly to your core values.

For instance, perhaps you remember a time you volunteered. The feeling of helping others, of making a tangible difference, might reveal a strong value of compassion or service. Or maybe you recall a moment of intense creative flow – painting, writing, composing music

– indicating a deep appreciation for creativity and self-expression. Alternatively, perhaps you remember the satisfaction of completing a challenging project at work, showcasing the value of competence and achievement.

Another method involves imagining your ideal life – not just the superficial aspects, but the underlying principles that would make it truly fulfilling. What kind of relationships would you have? What kind of work would you do? What kind of impact would you make on the world? Consider the qualities and characteristics that define this ideal life; these often reflect your deeply held values. Perhaps your ideal life involves close, intimate relationships, reflecting the value of connection and intimacy. Maybe it involves contributing to a cause you deeply believe in, suggesting a value of social justice or environmental sustainability. Or maybe it centers around intellectual exploration and constant learning, suggesting a value of knowledge and growth.

DON'T BE AFRAID TO CHALLENGE YOUR ASSUMPTIONS.

What you *think* your values are may not necessarily align with your actions. We often tell ourselves we value certain things – honesty, for example – but our behavior might betray a different reality.

A critical step is to honestly examine your actions and choices.

Do your actions consistently reflect the values you claim to hold? If not, it's time for some honest reflection.

Why is there a discrepancy?

Are there external pressures preventing you from living in alignment with your true values?

LET'S CONSIDER SOME EXAMPLES OF COMMON CORE VALUES:

FAMILY & RELATIONSHIPS: The importance of strong, loving connections with family and friends. This value often manifests in prioritizing time spent with loved ones, actively nurturing relationships, and valuing loyalty and support.

HEALTH & WELL-BEING: Prioritizing physical and mental health through healthy habits, mindful living, and self-care. This value might lead to regular exercise, healthy eating, and mindful practices like meditation or yoga.

CREATIVITY & SELF-EXPRESSION: The desire to create, innovate, and express oneself authentically through various means. This could manifest in artistic pursuits, writing, music, or even in the way you approach your work.

LEARNING & GROWTH: A commitment to continuous learning, personal development, and expanding one's knowledge and understanding. This value often translates into pursuing further education, engaging in intellectual pursuits, and embracing new experiences.

FINANCIAL SECURITY: The importance of financial stability and providing for oneself and one's family. This value could drive career choices, financial planning, and a focus on resourcefulness.

CONTRIBUTION & SERVICE: The desire to contribute to something larger than oneself, to make a positive impact on the world. This often involves volunteering, philanthropic work, or pursuing a career that aligns with a social cause.

ADVENTURE & EXPLORATION: A desire for new experiences, travel, and a sense of excitement and discovery. This value often manifests in a willingness to step outside of one's comfort zone, embrace change, and seek new challenges.

INTEGRITY & HONESTY: The commitment to living with integrity, honesty, and ethical conduct. This value drives decision-making, shapes relationships, and dictates behavior in all aspects of life.

FREEDOM & INDEPENDENCE: The desire for autonomy, self-reliance, and the freedom to make one's own choices. This might lead to pursuing entrepreneurial endeavors, prioritizing personal freedom, and resisting undue pressure from external forces.

SPIRITUALITY & PURPOSE: The search for meaning, purpose, and connection to something greater than oneself. This value can manifest in religious or spiritual practices, philosophical inquiry, or simply a deep sense of purpose in life.

These are just a few examples; your own core values may be different, and that's perfectly fine. The important thing is to identify the principles that genuinely resonate with you, the values that guide your decisions and shape your sense of self.

Once you've identified your core values, the next step is to examine how your actions align with those values. Are you living in congruence with your beliefs? Often, we find ourselves drifting away from our true values due to external pressures, fear of failure, or simply a lack of awareness. But by actively aligning our actions with our values, we create a more authentic and fulfilling life.

This process involves conscious decision-making. When faced with a choice, ask yourself: "Does this decision align with my core values?" If the answer is no, consider the implications. Is it worth sacrificing your values for short-term gain or to please others? Often, the answer will be a resounding no. Living authentically means making choices that reflect who you truly are.

REMEMBER, THIS JOURNEY ISN'T ABOUT PERFECTION; IT'S ABOUT PROGRESS.

You're not expected to seamlessly align your actions with your values overnight. There will be times when you stumble, when you make choices that don't fully align with your beliefs. The key is to acknowledge these moments, learn from them, and course-correct as needed. Self-compassion is crucial in this process. Be kind to yourself, recognize that you're human, and forgive yourself for imperfections.

Identifying your core values is not a one-time event; it's an ongoing process. As you grow and evolve, your values may shift and deepen. Regularly revisit this exercise, reflecting on your life experiences and re-evaluating your core beliefs. This ongoing process of self-discovery is essential to navigating life's complexities and living a truly fulfilling life. Your values are your compass, guiding you toward a life that is authentically yours. Embrace the journey, trust your intuition, and allow your values to be the driving force behind your decisions and actions. The path to a meaningful life begins with understanding the inner compass that guides you.

Your values are the stars in your soul's sky, a celestial map guiding you through life's ever-changing currents toward your true north.

VALUES CLARIFICATION EXERCISE

Now that we've established the profound importance of identifying your core values, let's move from theoretical understanding to practical application. This section focuses on exercises designed to help you unearth, clarify, and ultimately integrate your values into your daily life. These aren't just abstract concepts; they're the building blocks of a life lived authentically and with purpose.

The first exercise involves a simple yet powerful act of reflection: **listing your values.** Grab a pen and paper, or open a new document on your computer. Don't overthink it; just let the words flow. Think about the moments in your life where you felt most alive, most fulfilled, most genuinely yourself. What qualities or principles were present in those situations? What did you prioritize? Write them down. Don't censor yourself; include everything that comes to mind, from the seemingly insignificant to the profoundly impactful. You might find yourself listing things like honesty, creativity, family, adventure, knowledge, kindness, freedom, or security. The list is personal and unique to you.

This initial list might feel somewhat haphazard. That's perfectly normal. The next step is to **refine your list**. Review your initial entries. Are there any duplicates? Can you group similar values together under a broader umbrella? For example, "helping others," "compassion," and "empathy" might all fall under the broader value of "kindness." This process of simplification will help you identify your core values—the foundational beliefs that truly underpin your life.

Your values are the whispers of your soul, the gentle nudges that remind you of who you are and what you stand for, your compass in a chaotic world.

Now, let's delve deeper. Consider the **hierarchy of your values**. Arrange your refined list in order of importance. Which values are non-negotiable for you? Which are more flexible, depending on the circumstances? This exercise illuminates which values are paramount in your life and which ones might be influenced by external pressures or societal expectations. This ranking isn't set in stone; it's a snapshot of your current understanding. Revisit this exercise periodically to see how your priorities shift over time.

The following exercise is designed to help you **distinguish between superficial and profound values.** We often confuse wants with values. A want might be a fancy car or a luxurious vacation; a value is something far deeper, something that gives your life meaning and purpose. To differentiate, ask yourself: "If I had everything I wanted materially, would this still be important to me?" If the answer is yes, it's likely a true value. If the answer is no, it's probably more of a want, a temporary desire that may fade with time. This distinction is crucial.

Building your life around wants leads to fleeting satisfaction; building it around values leads to lasting fulfillment.

Let's explore this further with some examples. Suppose someone lists "wealth" as a value. Is this a profound value, or is it a reflection of a deeper need for security or independence? Digging deeper might reveal that the true underlying value is actually security or self-sufficiency. Similarly, someone who lists "popularity" might be masking a deeper need for connection, belonging, or love. Understanding this distinction is paramount to living a life aligned with your true self.

Now, we'll address a crucial aspect of values clarification: **values in conflict**. Inevitably, you will encounter situations where your values clash. For example, you might value both honesty and protecting your friend's feelings. How do you navigate this conflict? There is no easy answer, but the process of acknowledging the conflict is the first step toward a thoughtful resolution. Consider the consequences of prioritizing one value over the other. What are the potential short-term and long-term effects of your decision? This exercise fosters self-awareness and encourages mindful decision-making. It reinforces the idea that life isn't about avoiding difficult choices but rather about making conscious, value-driven choices.

To further explore this concept, let's use a hypothetical scenario. Imagine you are offered a lucrative job opportunity that requires you to relocate far from your family. You highly value both career advancement and strong family ties. This presents a direct conflict. To resolve this, you might consider the following questions: How important is career advancement to my overall happiness? How important is maintaining close relationships with my family? What compromises are possible? Can I find a way to balance both values, perhaps by maintaining frequent communication with family through technology or visiting regularly? The act of consciously weighing these factors helps you make a decision aligned with your deepest values, even when those values pull you in opposing directions.

The next exercise focuses on **values in action**. Once you've identified your core values, the real work begins: integrating them into your daily life. Start by consciously making decisions that reflect your values. For example, if you value honesty, strive to be truthful in all your interactions, even when it's difficult. If you value kindness, make an effort to show compassion to others, both in your personal and professional life. This constant practice of aligning your actions with your values strengthens their influence on your life and reinforces your sense of self.

Let's consider some practical applications. If you value creativity, actively seek out opportunities to express your creative side, whether it's through painting, writing, or any other artistic pursuit. If you value learning, commit to regular self-improvement, whether through reading, taking courses, or exploring new subjects. If you value physical health, incorporate regular exercise and healthy eating into your routine.

These small, consistent actions will gradually shape your life into a reflection of your core values. It's through consistent action that values transform from abstract concepts into the very fabric of your being.

The final exercise involves **seeking feedback**. Share your clarified values with trusted friends or family members. Ask them if your actions align with the values you've identified. Their perspectives can offer valuable insights you might have overlooked. Sometimes, we are blind to our own inconsistencies. Constructive feedback from others can help you identify areas where you can improve the alignment between your values and your actions. This feedback is invaluable for continuous growth and self-awareness. It serves as a powerful check and balance to ensure you stay true to your core principles.

Your values may evolve over time, and that's perfectly fine. Regularly revisit these exercises, allowing for reflection and adjustment as your life experiences shape and deepen your understanding of yourself. The process of self-discovery is an ongoing, dynamic one. Embrace the journey, learn from your experiences, and allow your values to be the guiding compass that steers you towards a life of authenticity and fulfillment. This journey of self-discovery is your own; embrace it and trust the process. Your unique values are not only your compass but also your anchor, grounding you amidst life's complexities and ensuring that you always stay true to your most authentic self. The path to a meaningful life is paved with self-awareness, understanding, and the unwavering commitment to living a life aligned with your deepest values.

Let your values be the architects of your choices, shaping your actions and defining your legacy, a compass that leads you to a life of meaning.

ALIGNING ACTIONS WITH VALUES

The journey of self-discovery doesn't end with the identification of your core values. Knowing what you hold dear is only half the battle; the real challenge lies in translating those values into your everyday actions. This is where the rubber meets the road, where the abstract concepts of integrity, compassion, or creativity become tangible choices in the architecture of your life. Without this alignment, your values remain beautiful ideals, dormant and unfulfilled, like a masterpiece left unfinished on an easel.

Imagine a ship with a finely tuned compass, pointing resolutely towards its desired destination. But what if the captain consistently ignores the compass, charting a course based on fleeting whims or external pressures? The vessel, despite possessing the navigational tools, will inevitably drift off course, likely never reaching its intended harbor. Similarly, knowing your values without acting on them leaves you adrift, unmoored from your true north.

The incongruence between values and actions creates an internal dissonance, a subtle yet persistent tension that manifests in various ways. You might experience a nagging feeling of unease, a sense that something is fundamentally amiss. Perhaps you feel a persistent low-level anxiety, a chronic dissatisfaction that resists easy explanation.

This dissonance can erode your self-esteem, leaving you questioning your own integrity and authenticity. It can lead to feelings of resentment, frustration, and even despair as the gap between your ideals and your reality widens.

Consider the individual who values family above all else, yet consistently prioritizes work, neglecting their loved ones. The disconnect between their professed value and their actions creates a rift, potentially damaging their relationships and leaving them feeling empty despite their professional success. Or the person who cherishes creativity but spends their days in a soul-crushing job that stifles their artistic expression. The unfulfilled potential festers, creating a sense of unlived life, a whisper of "what if?" that persistently haunts their waking hours.

Allow your values to be the wind in your sails, propelling you forward on the journey of life, a compass that ensures you reach your destination with integrity and grace.

Aligning your actions with your values is not simply about making grand gestures or dramatic life changes. It's about making conscious choices, day in and day out, that reflect your deepest convictions. It's about the small, seemingly insignificant decisions that collectively shape the trajectory of your life. It's the choice to spend an extra fifteen minutes talking to a friend instead of rushing through a to-do list, choosing kindness over convenience, investing time in a hobby that nourishes your soul rather than pursuing an activity that only pays the bills. It's about consistently choosing your values, your compass, over the seductive pull of societal expectations or the fleeting allure of instant gratification.

How then, do we bridge this gap between our values and our actions? The process is often gradual, requiring conscious effort, self-awareness, and a willingness to confront uncomfortable truths. It starts with honest self-reflection.

Examine your daily routine, scrutinizing your choices and identifying areas where there's a discrepancy between your stated values and your actual behavior.

Where are you compromising your principles?

Where are you neglecting your values in favor of immediate gratification or external pressure?

Be brutally honest with yourself. Avoid the temptation to rationalize or justify your inconsistencies. Honest self-assessment is the cornerstone of this process. Ask yourself: What are the obstacles that prevent me from aligning my actions with my values? Are these obstacles rooted in fear, insecurity, or lack of self-belief? Are there external pressures, societal expectations, or ingrained habits that are pulling me away from my true north? Once you've identified the obstacles, you can begin to address them, developing strategies to overcome them.

This process isn't about achieving unattainable perfection. It's about striving for congruence, recognizing that you are a work in progress and that setbacks are inevitable. It's okay to make mistakes, to stumble and fall. The critical aspect is to acknowledge those slip-ups, learn from them, and get back on track. Self-compassion is crucial. Do not beat yourself up over minor inconsistencies. Focus on the progress, not the perfection.

Your values are the roots that anchor you in the storms of life, providing the strength and stability to navigate any challenge, your personal compass towards resilience.

One effective strategy is to establish a system of accountability. Sharing your values and goals with trusted friends or family members can provide a support system and encourage you to stay committed to your chosen path. Consider working with a coach or therapist who can help you navigate this process, providing guidance and support as you work towards aligning your actions with your values. The external accountability can be incredibly helpful in overcoming inertia and staying focused on your goals.

Another powerful tool is the practice introspection. Paying attention to your thoughts, feelings, and actions in the present moment enables you to become more aware of your choices and their implications. Mindfulness cultivates self-awareness, allowing you to identify patterns of behavior that contradict your values, providing you with the opportunity to make conscious, more value-aligned choices.

Visualizing your ideal self, the person who consistently embodies your values, can also be helpful. Spend time imagining what your life would look like if your actions were perfectly aligned with your beliefs. What would you be doing? How would you feel? How would you interact with others? This visualization process can serve as a powerful motivator, providing a clear vision of the life you aspire to create.

Break down your large-scale goals into smaller, more manageable steps. Rather than trying to overhaul your entire life overnight, focus on small, incremental changes that move you steadily towards your desired state of alignment. Celebrate these small victories, reinforcing positive behaviors and maintaining momentum.

For instance, if your core value is health, start by incorporating a single healthy habit into your daily routine, like drinking a glass of water each morning. Once this becomes ingrained, add another, like a brief exercise session. This gradual approach makes the process less overwhelming and more sustainable in the long run. Remember, aligning your actions with your values is a lifelong journey, not a destination.

Finally, remember the power of forgiveness. If you stumble, if you deviate from your intended path, don't let self-criticism derail your progress. Instead, acknowledge your missteps, learn from them, and forgive yourself. Self-compassion is crucial in maintaining momentum on this long-term journey of self-discovery and self-alignment. Embrace the process, celebrate your progress, and allow your values to be the guiding star illuminating your path towards a life of authenticity and fulfillment.

The journey is the destination, and each step taken in alignment with your values is a step towards a more meaningful and authentic existence. This is not just about self-improvement; it's about self-realization. It's about becoming the person you were meant to be. It is a courageous and transformative endeavor, worthy of your unwavering commitment and persistent effort. Embrace the journey, for it is in this very journey that you will discover not only who you want to be, but, even more profoundly, who you already are.

VALUES AS A GUIDE FOR DECISION MAKING

Building on the foundation of understanding your core values, we now enter the crucial phase of integrating them into your decision-making process. This isn't about creating a rigid rulebook; it's about cultivating a mindful approach to choices, large and small, ensuring they resonate with your deepest sense of self. Think of your values as a compass, constantly guiding you towards your true north, even when the terrain is challenging and the path ahead is unclear.

Let's start with a practical exercise. Consider a recent decision you made – perhaps choosing a career path, selecting a romantic partner, or even deciding what to eat for dinner. Now, analyze that decision through the lens of your identified values. Did your choice align with your sense of purpose, integrity, or compassion? Or did it feel like a compromise, a deviation from your inner compass? This reflective process allows you to identify patterns in your decision-making, highlighting areas where your actions consistently reflect your values and areas where discrepancies might exist.

Identifying these discrepancies is not a condemnation of past choices. It's an opportunity for growth and self-awareness. Understanding where your actions fell short of your values can illuminate blind spots and help you recalibrate your approach to future decisions. For instance, if you value creativity but consistently choose work that stifles your imagination, this exercise will reveal an important dissonance you can start addressing. Perhaps it's time to explore alternative career paths, even if that requires a leap of faith and stepping outside your comfort zone.

The key here is to approach this self-reflection with kindness and compassion.

Life is complex, and we don't always have the luxury of making choices that perfectly align with all our values in every situation. Compromise is inevitable, but the aim is to minimize those compromises and strive for alignment as much as possible. *The goal isn't perfection; it's progress.*

Consider the concept of "value conflict." This arises when multiple values clash, creating an internal tug-of-war. For example, you might value both family and career advancement, yet a demanding job might require sacrifices in family time. Navigating these conflicts requires careful consideration and thoughtful prioritization. There's no easy answer, but a framework for exploring these conflicts can be exceptionally useful. This may involve weighing the long-term implications of each choice, considering the potential consequences of each path, and seeking support from trusted friends or mentors to gain external perspectives. Ultimately, the decision you make should be one that feels authentic to you, even if it isn't perfect.

One effective method for navigating value conflicts is the "weighted values" approach. List your conflicting values, assigning a numerical weight to each based on their relative importance to you in this specific situation. This isn't a rigid formula; it's a subjective process designed to bring clarity to the internal debate. By acknowledging the differing weights of your values, you can then begin to evaluate your options more thoughtfully and determine which decision best respects the hierarchy you've established.

Another invaluable tool is the practice of mindful decision-making. This involves slowing down, taking a deep breath, and consciously considering your values before making a choice. This mindful pause allows you to step back from the immediate urgency of the situation, allowing you to access a clearer perspective, unburdened by impulse or emotional reactivity. Incorporating mindfulness into your decision-making process helps you to approach choices with intention and awareness, increasing the likelihood that the outcome aligns with your authentic self.

This principle extends beyond major life decisions. Mindful decision-making applies equally to the small, seemingly inconsequential choices we make every day. What do you eat? How do you spend your free time? Who do you choose to spend time with? Even seemingly trivial choices, when made consistently in alignment with your values, contribute to a life that feels more authentic and fulfilling. Every "yes" and "no" becomes a statement of your values, reinforcing your commitment to living a life congruent with your deepest aspirations.

Let your values be the compass in your hand, the unwavering guide that leads you to the shores of a life lived with purpose and integrity.

Let's look at some specific examples. Imagine you're offered a lucrative job that requires long hours and frequent travel. If you value family time and work-life balance, this offer might present a conflict. A mindful approach would involve weighing the financial benefits against the potential strain on your relationships and well-being. If you value personal growth and professional development, you might find yourself re-evaluating your priorities and determining if the job's long hours are worth the challenges. The act of weighing your options based on the significance of your values is the key to making a decision that feels both rational and authentic.

Similarly, consider the situation of choosing a romantic partner. If you value honesty and integrity, you'll seek a partner who embodies those qualities. If you value emotional connection and intimacy, you'll prioritize building a relationship founded on trust and mutual respect. These values act as filters, helping you discern which relationships are aligned with your needs and which are not. The crucial part is recognizing that choosing a partner based on your values doesn't mean settling for less, but rather choosing a relationship likely to bring lasting happiness and fulfillment.

Beyond romantic relationships, your values should guide you in your friendships and social interactions. If you value loyalty and support, you'll prioritize nurturing those relationships that reciprocate this commitment. If you value authenticity and honesty, you'll surround yourself with people who encourage you to be your true self, without judgment or pretense. The decisions you make about your social circle are just as important as the choices you make in your professional and personal life, all contributing to the overall fabric of your authentic existence.

The process of using your values as a decision-making compass isn't static; it's an ongoing journey of self-discovery and refinement. As you navigate life's challenges and celebrate its triumphs, your values might evolve and deepen, or you might gain a more nuanced understanding of their interrelationships. This is perfectly normal, and it underscores the dynamic nature of self-awareness. Regularly reviewing and reflecting on your values helps ensure your compass remains true and your decisions continue to reflect your authentic self.

The most powerful decisions are born from the quiet conviction of your values, creating a life where your actions speak louder than words.

Remember that this process of aligning your decisions with your values isn't about achieving flawless consistency. Life inevitably throws curveballs, presenting unexpected challenges that may require you to make difficult choices, even those that temporarily deviate from your ideal alignment. The crucial element is your intentionality and commitment to returning to that alignment as quickly as possible. Don't be discouraged by occasional missteps; embrace them as learning opportunities and use them to refine your understanding of your values and how they guide you toward living a life that is both authentic and meaningful. Your values are not a rigid code, but rather a flexible framework that provides guidance and support as you navigate the complexities of life. The journey of self-discovery is an ongoing process, and using your values as your compass is essential to finding your true north and living a life aligned with your deepest self.

When your decisions harmonize with your values, you create a life of unwavering peace, knowing that you are walking your true path.

REDEFINING SUCCESS BEYOND EXTERNAL VALIDATION

We've spent a considerable time exploring your core values, the internal compass guiding your journey. Now, let's address a critical aspect often overlooked in the pursuit of a fulfilling life: redefining success. For many, success is equated with external markers: wealth, status, accolades, and social approval. These are often the metrics society uses to measure achievement, the benchmarks against which we unconsciously judge ourselves and others. But what happens when you achieve these external markers, yet feel a profound sense of emptiness, a gnawing dissatisfaction that no amount of material possessions or social recognition can fill?

This is where the critical shift occurs. The pursuit of externally defined success often leads to a life lived for others, a constant striving for validation that leaves you feeling perpetually depleted and unfulfilled. It's a treadmill of achievement, chasing the next milestone without ever truly appreciating the journey or the person you've become along the way. It's a life lived in reaction to external pressures, rather than in response to your inner voice.

My own journey profoundly illuminated this truth. For years, I measured my success by the quantifiable: prestigious titles, professional accomplishments, and the accumulation of material wealth. I relentlessly pursued these markers, believing they were the keys to happiness and fulfillment. But the more I achieved, the emptier I felt. The hollow echo of accomplishment reverberated within, a stark reminder that external validation is a fleeting and ultimately unsatisfying pursuit. It was only when I began to examine my own values, to prioritize inner peace and genuine connection over external validation, that I discovered a deeper, more profound sense of success.

This isn't to say that achieving goals and recognizing accomplishments is inherently wrong. Quite the contrary. Setting goals and working towards them can be incredibly motivating and rewarding. However, the crucial distinction lies in *why* you are pursuing these goals.

Are you driven by an internal desire to grow, learn, and contribute something meaningful to the world?

Or are you motivated by a need for external approval, a desperate attempt to prove your worth to others?

The answer to this question is the key to understanding your true relationship with success.

The most profound victories are those won within the sanctuary of your own heart, where validation comes not from others, but from the deep resonance of your authentic self.

Consider the classic scenario: the high-powered executive who boasts a six-figure salary, a luxurious home, and a prestigious position, yet feels a deep sense of loneliness and unfulfillment. This person has achieved what many would consider the pinnacle of success, yet they lack a fundamental connection to their own values and their true purpose. This disconnect creates a void that no amount of material wealth or professional achievement can ever fill.

Redefining success means consciously choosing to measure your life against your *own* internal compass. It means aligning your actions with your values, ensuring that your daily choices reflect your deepest aspirations and beliefs. It's about cultivating a sense of purpose and meaning that stems from within, rather than relying on external sources of validation.

HOW DO WE MAKE THIS SHIFT?

It's a gradual process of self-discovery and mindful intention. Begin by asking yourself these crucial questions:

WHAT TRULY MATTERS TO ME?

What are the core values that guide my decisions and shape my interactions with the world? Consider your relationships, your work, your personal interests – what truly nourishes your soul?

WHAT BRINGS ME JOY AND A SENSE OF PURPOSE?

What activities make me feel alive, engaged, and passionate? These activities are often linked to your core values and indicate areas where you can cultivate a more fulfilling life.

WHAT IMPACT DO I WANT TO HAVE ON THE WORLD?

What contribution can I make that aligns with my values and brings me a sense of meaning? Focusing on contribution shifts the emphasis from self-centered achievement to a more expansive and fulfilling purpose.

WHAT DOES SUCCESS LOOK LIKE TO ME, INDEPENDENT OF SOCIETAL EXPECTATIONS?

Free yourself from the constraints of conventional definitions. Success is not a one-size-fits-all concept. It's a deeply personal and evolving definition shaped by your unique values and experiences.

Once you've honestly answered these questions, you'll gain a clearer picture of your own personalized definition of success. It might involve achieving specific goals, but it will also encompass a broader sense of well-being, fulfillment, and contribution. It might involve financial security, but it will also prioritize strong relationships, personal growth, and a sense of purpose. It will be a definition unique to you, a reflection of your own intrinsic values and aspirations.

This process requires courage. It demands that you challenge societal norms and the deeply ingrained beliefs you may have absorbed about what constitutes a "successful" life. It requires the willingness to question your assumptions, to confront your fears, and to embrace a path that may deviate from the well-worn road of conventional success. But the rewards are immeasurable. A life lived in alignment with your values is a life lived with purpose, authenticity, and joy, regardless of the external accolades it may or may not garner.

Consider the artist who dedicates their life to their craft, even if financial success remains elusive. Their success lies in the expression of their creativity, the creation of art that touches the hearts and minds of others, the fulfillment derived from pursuing their passion. Or the teacher who dedicates their life to inspiring the next generation, finding their success in the growth and development of their students, in the positive impact they make on their lives, not in monetary compensation.

These examples highlight a different kind of success, one that transcends material wealth and social status. It's a success born of purpose, driven by intrinsic motivation, and measured by the impact you have on the world and your own sense of well-being. This type of success is sustainable, resilient, and deeply fulfilling. It's a success that nourishes your soul and provides a sense of lasting meaning.

The path towards redefining success is a continuous journey of self-discovery. It requires ongoing reflection, mindful decision-making, and the courage to live a life authentic to your own values. It's a journey of aligning your external actions with your internal compass, ensuring that your life is a reflection of your deepest self, a proof of the person you truly are meant to be. Don't be afraid to deviate from the prescribed paths, to forge your own trail, to define success on your own terms. Your authentic success awaits you. Embrace it. Live it. Own it. The journey may have its challenges, but the destination, the profound sense of fulfillment derived from a life lived authentically, is worth every step of the way. Remember, true success isn't a destination, but a continuous unfolding, a reflection of your ongoing commitment to living a life aligned with your deepest values and truest self. This is where you find not only success, but true and lasting happiness. The journey itself, with all its twists and turns, becomes a testimony to the strength and resilience you discover within. And that, my friend, is a success beyond measure.

The journey of redefining success is a continuous exploration of our inner landscape, a process of uncovering our deepest desires and aligning our actions with our authentic selves. It is a journey of self-discovery that unfolds with each step, each challenge, each triumph.

DISCOVERING YOUR PASSIONS

IGNITE YOUR INNER FIRE

UNCOVERING HIDDEN TALENTS AND INTERESTS

Discovering hidden passions and talents often feels like searching for a buried treasure. We may have glimpses, fleeting moments of intense engagement or satisfaction, that hint at something deeper within us, yet we often dismiss these as mere hobbies or coincidences.

The truth is, that many of our deepest passions and talents lie dormant, obscured by self-doubt, societal expectations, or simply a lack of exploration.

This section is dedicated to unearthing those hidden gems, guiding you on a journey of self-discovery that will illuminate your unique strengths and ignite your inner fire.

The first step in uncovering hidden talents and interests involves a deep dive into introspection.

Think back to your childhood. What activities did you lose yourself in? What sparked your curiosity and ignited your imagination? Were you a natural storyteller, captivating your friends with elaborate tales? Did you spend hours building intricate structures with LEGOs or lost in the world of drawing and painting? These early passions often foreshadow the talents that may lie dormant within us. Take a moment to recall those moments. Jot down a list of activities you enjoyed as a child, and consider what skills or interests they might have cultivated. Don't judge yourself; simply observe and record.

This process of revisiting childhood memories is just the beginning. We need to move beyond nostalgia and explore the present. What activities do you find yourself drawn to even now, despite your busy schedule or other commitments? Do you find yourself gravitating towards specific genres of books, movies, or music? Do you secretly wish you had more time to pursue a particular skill, hobby, or creative endeavor? Perhaps you're fascinated by astronomy, captivated by photography, or drawn to the intricate art of calligraphy. These are all clues, subtle hints pointing towards hidden passions that deserve nurturing.

One effective method for uncovering hidden interests is to explore new experiences. Step outside your comfort zone and try something entirely new. Take a pottery class, join a hiking group, attend a cooking workshop, learn a new language, or volunteer for a cause that resonates with you. By exposing yourself to different activities and environments, you increase the likelihood of discovering something that unexpectedly ignites your passion. The key is to approach these experiences with an open mind and a willingness to embrace the unknown. Don't be afraid to experiment and try different things until you find something that resonates with you on a deeper level.

Another powerful technique involves identifying your strengths and weaknesses. While understanding our weaknesses is crucial for personal growth, our strengths often hold the key to unlocking our hidden talents. What are you naturally good at? What do you consistently receive compliments on? What tasks or activities do you find yourself effortlessly excelling at? These strengths often represent areas where we have untapped potential waiting to be explored. Once you've identified your strengths, consider how you could leverage them in new and unexpected ways. Could your organizational skills be applied to a project management role? Could your creative writing abilities be utilized to write a blog or even a novel? The possibilities are endless.

The obstacle to uncovering your brilliance isn't a lack of stars within, but the clouds of self-doubt that obscure their light. Dispel the clouds, and your talents will illuminate the world.

Often, the obstacle to uncovering hidden talents isn't a lack of potential, but rather a lack of belief in ourselves. We may dismiss our abilities as insignificant or irrelevant, convinced that we lack the necessary skills or experience. This self-doubt stems from limiting beliefs that we've internalized over time. These beliefs can be deeply ingrained, hindering our ability to recognize and pursue our true passions.

To overcome these limiting beliefs, we must engage in a conscious effort to challenge and reframe our negative thoughts.

Ask yourself:

"What evidence supports this belief?"

"What would happen if I believed the opposite?"

By systematically challenging these limiting beliefs, we can begin to cultivate a more positive and empowering self-image, opening ourselves up to the possibility of discovering and pursuing our hidden talents.

Consider the example of a person who always loved music but believed they lacked the talent to play an instrument. They may have dismissed their passion, focusing on more "practical" pursuits. However, if they were to challenge their limiting belief – "I'm not musical enough" – they might realize that their love for music transcends mere performance. They might discover a passion for music production, songwriting, or even music journalism, all fulfilling their inherent passion in a way they never considered.

Another crucial aspect in discovering hidden talents lies in identifying your values. What truly matters to you? What principles guide your decisions and shape your worldview? Understanding your values can provide a framework for identifying passions that align with your deepest beliefs. If you value creativity, for instance, you might find fulfillment in pursuing artistic endeavors like painting, sculpting, or writing. If you value helping others, you might discover a passion for social work, volunteering, or teaching. By aligning your passions with your values, you create a sense of purpose and fulfillment that extends beyond mere enjoyment.

The map to your hidden talents is etched in the language of self-belief. Learn to read it, and you will discover the uncharted territories of your extraordinary potential.

Self-discovery is an organic process, unfolding in unpredictable and often surprising ways. There will be moments of doubt, frustration, and even failure. It's crucial to embrace these experiences as opportunities for learning and growth. Don't be discouraged by setbacks; rather, view them as stepping stones on your path towards self-realization. Celebrate your small victories and learn from your mistakes. Remember that the process of uncovering hidden talents is an ongoing journey, not a destination. The more you explore, the more you'll discover about yourself and the unique potential that lies within.

Remember the power of community. Surround yourself with supportive friends, family, and mentors who encourage your exploration and celebrate your progress.

Share your aspirations with others and seek feedback on your endeavors. A supportive network can provide invaluable guidance, motivation, and inspiration as you embark on this transformative journey of self-discovery.

Don't be afraid to seek out resources, workshops, or mentors who can help you refine your skills and develop your talents. The path to uncovering your hidden passions may not always be easy, but the rewards are immeasurable. The journey itself is a confirmation of your courage, resilience, and commitment to living a life aligned with your truest self. Embrace the adventure, and allow yourself the freedom to explore the vast landscape of your own potential. The world awaits the unique contribution only you can make.

The treasure you seek lies within; the journey to find it is your greatest adventure yet.

EXPLORING CREATIVE OUTLETS

Uncovering our passions often feels like peeling back layers of an onion, each layer revealing a new facet of ourselves. We've touched upon the importance of introspection and identifying those fleeting moments of joy and engagement that hint at deeper desires. Now, let's delve into the practical steps of nurturing these nascent passions and channeling them into creative outlets. The beauty of creative expression lies in its ability to bridge the gap between our inner world and the outer world, allowing us to manifest our passions into tangible forms.

One of the most effective ways to connect with our inner passions is through creative exploration. This doesn't necessarily require possessing exceptional artistic talent; rather, it's about embracing the process of self-expression. Think about the activities that once brought you immense joy as a child—painting, sculpting, writing poetry, playing music, building things with Lego. These seemingly simple activities often hold the key to our deeper creative potential.

Perhaps you remember the sheer delight of creating a magnificent sandcastle on the beach, meticulously crafting its towers and moats. That same meticulousness, that same intense focus, could be channeled into other creative pursuits as an adult. Perhaps it's time to rediscover the joy of sculpting, perhaps with clay this time, or building intricate models, perhaps of miniature landscapes. The materials may change, but the fundamental creative impulse remains.

Similarly, if you reveled in the magic of storytelling as a child, whether through elaborate fantasy worlds or simple tales of everyday adventures, explore writing again. It could be journaling, poetry, short stories, even a blog. The act of writing itself, of giving form to your thoughts and experiences, can be profoundly therapeutic and revelatory. It's a way to unpack your emotions, to understand yourself better, and to connect with your authentic voice. Don't worry about perfection; the goal is to express yourself, not to impress anyone.

Let's say your childhood passion was music. Did you love singing, playing an instrument, or simply listening to music with deep absorption? Rekindle that connection. Perhaps you could take up singing lessons, dust off that old guitar, or even start creating your own playlists that reflect your current moods and aspirations. The act of creating a playlist can be surprisingly insightful. What themes emerge? What feelings do the songs evoke? These are important clues.

If you feel a lack of inspiration or direction, don't despair. Explore different creative outlets. Try painting, even if you haven't held a brush since school. Take a pottery class, even if the only thing you've ever sculpted is a snowman. Attend a writing workshop, even if the thought of sharing your work feels terrifying. The crucial step is to simply start. The process itself will guide you towards what resonates most deeply. Remember, the goal isn't to become the next Picasso or Hemingway; the goal is to tap into your innate creativity and connect with the joy of self-expression.

Many people find that combining different creative outlets amplifies the benefits. For example, someone passionate about nature photography might also enjoy writing descriptive captions for their images, or creating a photo book detailing their experiences. This merging of skills creates a more profound and rewarding experience, weaving together different strands of passion.

Don't underestimate the power of play. Embrace the childlike curiosity and freedom from judgment that you once possessed. Allow yourself to experiment, to make mistakes, to embrace imperfection. The creative process is about exploration, not about producing a masterpiece. Often, it's in those unexpected moments of playful exploration that we stumble upon our most authentic selves and our deepest passions. It's about the process, not the product.

The creative journey is a dance, not a battle. It's a winding path of discovery, with twists, turns, and moments of intense self-doubt. Don't race the muse. Let inspiration guide you. It's okay to feel lost or overwhelmed at times. It's okay to change course, to abandon one creative outlet and embrace another. The important thing is to keep moving forward, to keep exploring, to keep allowing yourself the freedom to express your unique creativity.

A powerful tool is seeking out a community of like-minded individuals. Join a writing group, a photography club, a painting class, or an online forum where you can connect with others who share your passion. Sharing your work and receiving constructive feedback can be incredibly motivating and transformative. The supportive environment can provide encouragement during moments of self-doubt and inspiration to push your creative boundaries further.

Remember that creative expression is not solely about artistic pursuits. It can also manifest in many other ways. Perhaps your passion lies in cooking, in designing spaces, in gardening, in organizing events, in teaching others. These are all forms of creative expression, each demanding imagination, ingenuity, and a unique approach. Find the avenues that allow you to express your creativity in ways that feel authentic and fulfilling.

If you're struggling to identify your creative outlets, try brainstorming activities that evoke a sense of flow. Flow, as described by Mihály Csikszentmihalyi, is a state of complete absorption in an activity, where time seems to disappear and you are fully present in the moment. Think about activities that bring you into that state of deep engagement. What sparks your curiosity? What challenges you in a positive way? What leaves you feeling energized and fulfilled?

Creative expression is not merely an act of making, but an act of becoming, a journey into the depths of your being, where your truest self is revealed.

Don't EVER limit your creative exploration to traditional art forms. Consider exploring unconventional creative outlets. Perhaps you find creative expression in building something, in coding, in problem-solving, in designing games, or in writing music. The possibilities are endless.

The key is to consistently engage in these creative activities, even if it's just for a few minutes each day. Consistency is crucial. Regular creative practice helps build momentum, strengthens your creative muscles, and creates a feedback loop that reinforces your passion and ignites your inner fire.

It's essential to remember that your creative journey is a personal one. There is no right or wrong way to express yourself. Don't compare your work to others; celebrate your unique voice and perspective. Embrace the imperfections, the mistakes, the moments of self-doubt. They are all part of the process. The journey itself is a tribute to your courage, your resilience, and your commitment to living a life aligned with your deepest self. The world awaits the unique contribution only you can make. The treasure you seek lies within; the journey to find it is your greatest adventure yet. Embrace the adventure, and allow yourself the freedom to explore the vast landscape of your own potential.

Allow your creative spirit to be the wild river that carves its own path, shaping the landscape of your life with the force of your imagination.

TURNING PASSION INTO PURPOSE

The journey from passion to purpose is not a sudden leap, but a gradual unfolding, a delicate dance between what ignites our soul and what gives our life meaning. It's a process of self-discovery, refinement, and unwavering commitment. We've explored the whispers of our passions, those moments of intense engagement that hint at our deeper desires. Now, let's transform those whispers into a resounding chorus, a life lived with intention and purpose.

The first step is understanding that passion isn't always glamorous. It's not always a dramatic revelation, a sudden burst of clarity. Often, it's a quiet hum beneath the surface, a persistent pull towards something we find inherently rewarding. It might be a love for crafting intricate details, a fascination with the intricacies of the human mind, and a deep empathy for those in need. These passions, seemingly small at first, are the seeds of purpose.

To cultivate these seeds, we must nurture them with intention. This means actively engaging with our passions, dedicating time and energy to explore them.

If you find joy in painting, don't let it be a weekend hobby; dedicate time each day, even if it's just for fifteen minutes. If you're drawn to helping others, seek volunteer opportunities, even if it's just a few hours a month. Consistent engagement strengthens the connection, deepening your understanding of your passion and its potential.

A crucial element in this process is aligning our passions with our values. What truly matters to us? What principles guide our decisions and shape our worldview? Our values provide the moral compass that guides our purpose. If compassion is a core value, for instance, pursuing a career in social work might be a natural progression of your passion for helping others. If creativity is paramount, exploring avenues for artistic expression might lead to a fulfilling purpose. This alignment provides a sense of integrity, ensuring our passions are not merely fleeting interests but deeply rooted convictions.

Setting realistic goals is another vital step. We must translate our passions into tangible objectives. Instead of simply saying, "I want to write a novel," a more realistic goal might be, "I will write 500 words every day for the next six months." Breaking down large aspirations into smaller, manageable steps makes the journey less daunting and more sustainable. Celebrate each milestone, however small, to build momentum and maintain motivation.

In the act of creation, you become a conduit for something larger than yourself, a vessel for the universal language of beauty, truth, and inspiration.

It's also essential to recognize that our passions might evolve over time. What ignites our soul today might shift in intensity or direction as we grow and learn. This is not a failure; it's a natural part of the journey. Flexibility and adaptability are key to staying aligned with our purpose. Be open to exploring new avenues, adjusting your goals as needed, and embracing the evolving nature of your passions.

You must consider the impact your passions might have on others. Purpose often involves contributing to something larger than ourselves, making a difference in the world.

Think about how your passions can serve others, creating positive change in your community or beyond.
This outward focus adds depth and meaning to your pursuit, transforming it from a personal endeavor into a shared journey.

Let's consider a few examples. Imagine Sarah, a talented musician who has always felt drawn to playing the cello. She initially sees this as a purely personal pursuit, a way to unwind and express her emotions. However, as she consistently practices and develops her skills, she realizes the profound impact her music has on others. She starts performing at nursing homes, bringing joy to the residents. Her passion, initially a private indulgence, evolves into a meaningful contribution to her community.

Or consider John, a software engineer with a passion for building user-friendly applications. He initially focuses on personal projects, honing his skills and exploring new technologies. He soon realizes that he can use his technical abilities to create apps that address social issues. He develops an application to connect volunteers with community organizations, thus transforming his passion into a powerful force for social good. John's passion for technology is no longer just a personal pursuit; it's a tool for creating positive change.

These examples highlight the transformative power of aligning passions with purpose. It's a journey of self-discovery, goal-setting, and continuous refinement. It's about understanding our values, identifying our talents, and leveraging them to create a life that is not only fulfilling but also meaningful. It is about contributing our unique gifts to the world, and weaving our passions into the fabric of our existence.

The path from passion to purpose is not always linear; it's rarely a straightforward ascent. There will be setbacks, moments of doubt, and periods of uncertainty. These challenges are not obstacles to be overcome, but rather opportunities for growth, learning, and deeper self-understanding. Embrace these moments; they are integral to the journey.

Remember to celebrate the small victories, acknowledge your progress, and continually reassess your path. Regular reflection is crucial. Ask yourself: *Am I still aligned with my values? Are my goals still relevant? Is my passion still burning brightly?* If the answers require adjustments, embrace the flexibility to modify your course.

The journey from passion to purpose is a lifelong endeavor, an ongoing process of growth and evolution. It's a journey of self-discovery, a dance between our inner world and the outer world, a celebration of our courage, our resilience, and our unwavering commitment to living a life that is both meaningful and authentic. Embrace the journey; the rewards are immeasurable. The world awaits your unique contribution. Your purpose awaits your discovery. And the journey of finding it is the most rewarding adventure you will ever embark on. Don't hesitate to seek guidance and support along the way; mentors, friends, and family can offer valuable insights and encouragement. Remember, you are not alone on this journey. The world is filled with individuals who understand and support the pursuit of a life lived with intention and purpose.

Creative expression is the courage to be vulnerable, to share the rawest parts of yourself with the world, and to invite others to connect through the shared language of art.

Allow yourself to be vulnerable. Share your passions with others; connect with like-minded individuals; build a supportive network. The shared experience of pursuing a purpose can be incredibly powerful and transformative. Your journey doesn't have to be a solitary one. And when you stumble, as you inevitably will, remember that it's okay to ask for help. It is a sign of strength, not weakness, to acknowledge your need for support. Embrace the imperfections, the setbacks, the moments of self-doubt, as they are all part of the process. The beauty lies in the journey itself. The growth, the evolution, the continuous refinement of your purpose. You are capable of achieving extraordinary things when you align your passions with your values and your goals. Embrace your journey, and let your unique purpose shine.

Vulnerability is the courageous act of shedding the armor of self-protection and allowing ourselves to be seen, truly seen, in all our imperfect glory.

OVERCOMING LIMITING BELIEFS

The walls of your limitations are built from the bricks of 'I can't.' demolish them with the unwavering declaration, 'I will.'

The whispers of your passions, the embers of your inner fire — we've explored how to identify them, how to nurture them. But often, a formidable wall stands between our desires and their realization: limiting beliefs. These are the insidious voices whispering doubts, the internal saboteurs that tell us we're not good enough, smart enough, or talented enough to pursue our dreams. They are the shackles that bind us to a life less lived, preventing us from igniting our inner fire and embracing our true potential.

These beliefs aren't born of malice; they're often rooted in past experiences, societal conditioning, and ingrained fears. Perhaps you faced criticism in the past, leading you to believe your passions are frivolous or unimportant. Maybe you've internalized societal expectations, convincing yourself that certain paths are more "acceptable" or "realistic" than others. Or perhaps the fear of failure looms large, paralyzing you before you even begin. Whatever their origin, limiting beliefs exert a powerful influence, subtly undermining our confidence and hindering our progress.

The first step in overcoming these beliefs is to identify them. Take some time for introspection. Ask yourself: What are the voices in my head telling me I can't do? What are the excuses I use to justify inaction? Write them down. Don't censor yourself; let the full force of these beliefs come to the surface. This act of acknowledging them is already a significant step toward dismantling their power. You are bringing these hidden saboteurs into the light, where they can be examined and challenged.

Once you've identified these beliefs, it's crucial to question their validity. Ask yourself: Is this belief actually true? What evidence supports it? What evidence contradicts it? Often, these beliefs are based on assumptions, fears, and past experiences that may no longer be relevant. Challenge the negativity by actively seeking out evidence to the contrary. Remember that past experiences don't define your future potential. You are capable of growth, adaptation, and exceeding your perceived limitations.

Let's consider some common limiting beliefs and how to dismantle them:

"I'M NOT TALENTED ENOUGH." This belief often stems from comparing ourselves to others, forgetting that everyone starts somewhere. Talent is not a fixed entity; it's a skill that can be developed and refined through practice, dedication, and learning. Think of your favorite musician, athlete, or artist. Did they achieve mastery overnight? No. They honed their skills through years of perseverance, overcoming countless setbacks and challenges. Your journey will be similar. Embrace the learning process, celebrate small victories, and focus on continuous improvement. Focus on the joy of the process, not just the end result.

"IT'S TOO LATE FOR ME TO PURSUE MY PASSIONS." Age is just a number. There's no expiration date on pursuing your dreams. Many people discover their passions later in life and achieve remarkable things. Consider the countless individuals who have made significant career changes or embarked on new adventures later in life. Their stories are proof of the resilience of the human spirit and the limitless possibilities that exist, regardless of age. The most important thing is to start. Today. Don't let the illusion of time wasted stop you from pursuing what truly matters. Remember, it's never too late to start living a life aligned with your passions.

"I'LL FAIL." The fear of failure is a universal human experience, but it shouldn't paralyze us. Failure is not the opposite of success; it's a stepping stone towards it. It's an opportunity to learn, grow, and adapt. Every setback is a chance to refine your approach, gain valuable insights, and emerge stronger. Embrace failure as a teacher, not a judge. Learn from your mistakes, adjust your strategy, and keep moving forward. Remember, persistence and resilience are key ingredients to success.

"I DON'T HAVE THE RESOURCES." Lack of resources can be a significant obstacle, but it's rarely insurmountable. Consider creative solutions: Can you learn new skills online? Can you find affordable alternatives? Can you collaborate with others to pool resources? Often, the greatest limitations are self-imposed. Explore different avenues, be resourceful, and remember that many successful individuals started with limited resources. Your creativity and determination will surprise you.

"WHAT WILL PEOPLE THINK?" This is a crippling belief that stems from a fear of judgment. The truth is, you can't control what others think, and you shouldn't let their opinions dictate your choices. Focus on living authentically and pursuing what brings you joy and fulfillment. The people who truly matter will support your journey. Their encouragement will far outweigh the negativity of those who don't understand.

Overcoming limiting beliefs is a continuous process, not a one-time event. It requires consistent self-reflection, challenging negative self-talk, and actively building self-belief. Develop positive affirmations, surround yourself with supportive people, celebrate your progress, and remember that you are capable of achieving remarkable things when you align your actions with your passions.

One effective technique is to reframe your negative thoughts. Instead of thinking, "I'm not good enough," reframe it as "I'm learning and improving every day." Instead of, "I'll fail," reframe it as "I'll learn from my mistakes and keep growing." This simple act of reframing can significantly shift your perspective and empower you to move forward.

Visualization is another powerful tool. Imagine yourself successfully pursuing your passions. Visualize the feeling of accomplishment, the sense of purpose, and the joy of living a life aligned with your values. The more vivid your visualization, the more powerful its effect on your subconscious mind.

Remember that self-compassion is crucial. Be kind to yourself throughout this process. Acknowledge your imperfections, celebrate your progress, and embrace the journey. Overcoming limiting beliefs is a marathon, not a sprint. There will be setbacks, and there will be moments of self-doubt, but your dedication to self-discovery will guide you towards your true potential. Keep moving forward, and watch as your inner fire ignites, illuminating the path toward a life filled with purpose, passion, and fulfillment. Embrace the journey, for it is within this unfolding process that you truly discover who you are meant to be.

Your potential is a vast, unmapped territory.
Limiting beliefs are false borders.
Erase them, and explore the boundless
landscape of your abilities.

THE POWER OF PERSISTENCE

Embarking on the journey of discovering and pursuing your passions is akin to scaling a mountain. The ascent isn't a smooth, effortless climb; it's punctuated by steep inclines, treacherous terrain, and unexpected storms. There will be moments when you question your ability to reach the summit, when doubt creeps in like a persistent shadow, whispering insidious suggestions of failure. But it is precisely these challenges, these moments of adversity, that forge resilience, deepen our understanding of ourselves, and ultimately, amplify the sweetness of victory.

Persistence isn't merely about pushing forward relentlessly; it's about cultivating a resilient spirit, a deep-seated belief in your capacity to overcome obstacles. It's about learning to view setbacks not as failures, but as valuable learning experiences, as stepping stones on the path to success. Each challenge encountered presents an opportunity for growth, a chance to refine your strategies, adjust your approach, and emerge stronger than before.

Think of a sculptor meticulously chiseling away at a block of marble. The process isn't instantaneous; it requires countless hours of focused effort, of painstaking attention to detail. There will be moments when the sculptor's hand slips, when a chip of marble breaks away unexpectedly. Yet, these imperfections don't deter the artist; they are part of the creative process, shaping the final masterpiece. Similarly, the setbacks we encounter on our journey toward realizing our passions are integral to our growth; they shape us, refining our skills and strengthening our resolve.

Remember the times you've faced adversity in other areas of your life. Perhaps you learned a new language, mastered a difficult skill, or overcame a personal challenge. Recall the persistence you demonstrated; the determination that propelled you forward despite setbacks. Draw upon these experiences as you navigate the pursuit of your passions; remember the strength you've already demonstrated, the resilience you already possess.

The path to our dreams is like a river, flowing through unexpected valleys and over unforeseen obstacles. We will encounter detours, unexpected roadblocks, and even moments where we feel utterly lost and discouraged.

These are not signs of failure; they are simply part of the journey. Learning to navigate these challenges, to adapt and persevere, is a crucial aspect of achieving lasting fulfillment. It's during these moments that we truly discover the depths of our own resilience, the power of our inner strength.

Consider the example of athletes who dedicate years of their lives to rigorous training. They don't achieve greatness without facing numerous setbacks — injuries, losses, periods of self-doubt. Yet, their persistence, their unwavering commitment to their goals, allows them to overcome these challenges and achieve extraordinary feats. Their success is not solely a result of talent; it's a confirmation of their resilience and unyielding dedication.

Similarly, artists, writers, entrepreneurs, and individuals pursuing any significant endeavor experience countless setbacks along the way. Rejected manuscripts, failed business ventures, creative blocks — these are all common experiences that can easily derail someone lacking the fortitude to persevere. But it is through embracing these challenges, learning from them, and adapting our approach that we ultimately find success.

The power of persistence lies not only in our ability to overcome obstacles but also in our capacity to learn from our mistakes. Every setback provides valuable feedback, offering insights into our strengths and weaknesses. It's a chance to analyze our strategies, identify areas for improvement, and refine our approach. This iterative process of learning, adapting, and refining is essential for long-term success. It's the essence of growth and progress.

Maintaining a positive mindset is crucial for sustained persistence. Cultivating optimism, focusing on the potential for success, and visualizing the achievement of our goals can significantly impact our motivation and perseverance. This doesn't mean ignoring the challenges; rather, it involves maintaining a balanced perspective, and acknowledging the difficulties while simultaneously focusing on the positive aspects of the journey.

Be kind to yourself, acknowledge your imperfections, and celebrate your progress, no matter how small. Avoid the trap of self-criticism, which can be debilitating and undermine your efforts. Instead, focus on your strengths, on the progress you've made, and on the lessons you've learned along the way. This positive self-talk will fuel your persistence and bolster your resilience.

It's also important to build a support network of like-minded individuals. Surround yourself with people who believe in you, and who offer encouragement and support during challenging times. Sharing your experiences, seeking advice, and celebrating your successes with others can provide invaluable emotional support and motivation. This network can serve as a buffer against self-doubt, providing encouragement and perspective when you need it most.

Another crucial element of persistence is the ability to break down large goals into smaller, more manageable steps. Facing an overwhelming task can be daunting and discouraging, leading to feelings of helplessness and a lack of motivation. However, by dividing the overall goal into smaller, more achievable milestones, you create a sense of progress and accomplishment, fostering a sense of momentum that keeps you moving forward.

Imagine the task of writing a novel. It can seem an insurmountable undertaking, but by breaking it down into chapters, scenes, and even individual paragraphs, the task becomes much more manageable. Celebrating the completion of each small milestone provides a sense of accomplishment, motivating you to continue the process. This technique works for virtually any ambitious goal.

True success often requires sustained effort and unwavering commitment. Persistence is a testament to the human spirit's capacity to overcome obstacles. There will be times when you feel overwhelmed, discouraged, and tempted to give up. But it is precisely during these moments that your resilience will be tested, your determination challenged. It is in these moments that you must remember why you started, the vision you hold for your future, and the unwavering commitment you have made to yourself.

The pursuit of your passions is a journey of self-discovery, a process of continuous growth and refinement. Embracing this journey, with all its challenges and triumphs, is crucial for achieving lasting fulfillment. It is in navigating the inevitable obstacles, in learning from our mistakes, and in persevering despite setbacks that we truly discover the strength and resilience within ourselves. The journey itself is a proof of your potential, a confirmation of the power of persistence. And the summit, when you finally reach it, will be all the more rewarding for the arduous climb. Embrace the journey, for it is within this unfolding process that you truly discover who you are meant to be.

The greatest act of liberation is to release yourself from the prison of 'I'm not enough.' You are more than you believe, and your potential is limitless.

DEFINING YOUR PURPOSE

GIVING MEANING TO YOUR LIFE

EXPLORE DIFFERENT APPROACHES TO DEFINING PURPOSE

The search for purpose is a deeply personal journey, a quest as unique as the individual undertaking it. There isn't a single, universally accepted definition, and thankfully so. What resonates profoundly with one person might feel utterly hollow to another. This inherent subjectivity is both the challenge and the beauty of this exploration. We'll examine various approaches, understanding that your definition of purpose will likely be a synthesis of these perspectives, molded to fit your unique life experiences, values, and aspirations.

Let's begin with the **spiritual and philosophical perspectives**. For many, purpose stems from a connection to something larger than themselves. This could be a belief in a higher power, a sense of interconnectedness with all beings, or a feeling of belonging to a universal consciousness. From this viewpoint, purpose isn't something you create; it's something you discover—a role preordained, a path already laid out, waiting for you to walk it. This perspective often emphasizes service to others, contributing to a greater good, and living a life aligned with universal principles of love, compassion, and wisdom. Think of the selfless dedication of a humanitarian worker, driven by a deep-seated belief in alleviating suffering and promoting human dignity. Or consider the artist inspired by a muse, channeling divine creativity onto canvas or through a musical instrument. Their purpose is a conduit for something transcendent, a reflection of a larger cosmic design. The challenge here lies in identifying your personal connection—your unique spiritual resonance—and translating that into tangible action in the everyday world.

Moving from the ethereal to the concrete, we encounter the **practical and action-oriented approaches**. This perspective emphasizes tangible goals, measurable outcomes, and demonstrable impact. Here, purpose isn't necessarily about grand philosophical concepts; it's about identifying your strengths, setting achievable goals, and making a difference in your chosen field. Perhaps your purpose lies in building a successful business that creates jobs and contributes to the economy. Or maybe it's about becoming a skilled professional who excels in your chosen career, using your expertise to solve problems and make a positive contribution to society. This approach often involves setting SMART goals—Specific, Measurable, Achievable, Relevant, and Time-bound—and consistently working towards their accomplishment. Success in this context is measurable, offering tangible evidence of progress and fulfillment. The challenge here is ensuring that your actions are not only productive but also aligned with your intrinsic values. Chasing external success alone, without a foundation of personal meaning, can leave you feeling unfulfilled, even if outwardly successful.

Another valuable approach draws from **psychology and positive psychology**, emphasizing well-being, personal growth, and self-actualization. This perspective posits that purpose is intrinsically linked to our overall happiness and flourishing. Identifying your purpose, therefore, becomes a process of understanding your strengths, weaknesses, values, and passions, and creating a life that allows you to leverage your strengths, overcome your weaknesses, live in accordance with your values, and pursue your passions. This involves self-reflection, mindfulness, and a willingness to embrace both challenges and successes as opportunities for learning and growth. The emphasis here is not on achieving a specific outcome but on cultivating a sense of purposefulness in your daily life – a feeling of being engaged, energized, and satisfied with your contributions to the world and to your own well-being. Tools such as journaling, meditation, and positive affirmations can facilitate this self-discovery process, helping you to identify what truly brings you joy, fulfillment, and a sense of meaning.

Beyond these broad categories, we can also explore more nuanced perspectives. Some people find purpose in **legacy-building**, striving to create something that will endure beyond their lifetime—a published work, a flourishing business, a family legacy. Others find it in **impact**, measuring their purpose through the difference they make in the lives of others. Still, others discover it in **personal mastery**, focusing on continuous self-improvement and the pursuit of excellence in their chosen field.

It's vital to remember that these are not mutually exclusive categories. Your purpose may well be a unique blend of spiritual conviction, practical achievement, personal growth, and legacy-building. A successful entrepreneur might find purpose in both the financial success of their business and its positive impact on their community. A dedicated teacher could experience purpose not only in educating students but also in the spiritual satisfaction of shaping young minds and fostering a love of learning. An artist might find purpose in the creative process itself, the impact their art has on others, and the enduring legacy it creates. The key is to explore these various lenses, allowing yourself to see your potential purpose from multiple angles, until a clear and resonant image emerges.

The process of defining your purpose isn't a one-time event; it's an ongoing evolution. As you grow and change, your understanding of your purpose will likely evolve as well. What resonates with you at age 25 might feel different at age 45. Life experiences, challenges, and triumphs will shape and reshape your understanding, leading you down unexpected paths and revealing new possibilities. Embracing this fluidity is key to avoiding rigidity and maintaining a sense of ongoing discovery and fulfillment.

Your purpose isn't a destination; it's a journey, a dynamic process of self-discovery and continuous growth. It's a compass that guides your choices, offering direction and meaning amidst life's complexities.

Don't EVER be afraid to experiment and explore. Try different approaches, consider various perspectives, and allow yourself the freedom to change course along the way. The most important thing is to begin the process, to engage in honest self-reflection, and to actively seek out what truly resonates within your heart and soul. The path to purpose is paved with self-discovery, and the rewards are immeasurable. It's a journey of continuous learning, growth, and the ever-unfolding revelation of your unique contribution to the world. This exploration requires courage, vulnerability, and a willingness to embrace the uncertainties inherent in the journey. But it's a journey well worth taking, one that leads to a life lived with authenticity, meaning, and profound fulfillment. The process itself is as valuable as the destination. Embrace the questions, the uncertainties, and the unexpected turns, for within them lies the potential for a life lived with purpose and profound personal satisfaction. The journey of self-discovery is a lifelong adventure, a masterfully crafted architecture where every layer is built from our experiences, reflections, and the ever-evolving understanding of who you are and what you are meant to be.

The most vibrant chapters of your story are written in the ink of exploration. Dare to venture beyond the familiar, and you will find your truest self in the unknown.

CONNECTING PURPOSE TO VALUES AND PASSIONS

Understanding the intricate dance between purpose, values, and passions is crucial in defining your own unique sense of meaning. These aren't separate entities existing in isolation; rather, they're interwoven threads forming the rich essence of a life lived with intention. Your values represent your core beliefs, the principles that guide your decisions and actions.

They act as the compass, pointing you towards the direction that feels authentically you. These values might include honesty, compassion, creativity, justice, or family – the list is as diverse and individual as the people who hold them. Take time to identify your core values. What truly matters to you, irrespective of external pressures or societal expectations? What principles would you defend, even at personal cost? Reflect on moments where you felt deeply satisfied and fulfilled; the values underpinning those experiences are likely key components of your personal compass.

Let your values be the foundation, your passions the fuel, and your purpose the guiding star. This is the alchemy of a life lived with profound meaning.

Passions, on the other hand, are the fuel that ignites your energy and enthusiasm. They're the activities that draw you in, captivating your attention and leaving you feeling energized and alive. These passions might be hobbies, skills, or areas of expertise that bring you joy and a sense of flow. Perhaps it's the thrill of artistic creation, the satisfaction of problem-solving, the connection fostered through community engagement, the tranquility found in nature, or the excitement of learning something new. The key is to distinguish between fleeting interests and genuine, deeply rooted passions. What truly excites you, leaving you feeling invigorated and wanting more? What activities make time seem to disappear, leaving you feeling utterly absorbed and present?

Purpose, then, arises from the intersection of your values and passions. It's the overarching aim that integrates your deepest beliefs with the activities that energize you. It's the 'why' behind your actions, the driving force that fuels your commitment and shapes your trajectory. Your purpose isn't simply a career or a role; it's a deeper sense of meaning and contribution, a feeling of alignment between your inner world and your outer actions. It answers the question: "What impact do I want to make on the world, reflecting my core values and utilizing my passions?"

Let's explore this interconnection through examples. Imagine someone whose core values are family, community, and creativity. Their passions might involve painting, writing, or music. Their purpose might then evolve into creating art that celebrates family life and builds community connections, perhaps through teaching art classes to children or organizing community art projects. In this scenario, their values guide their choices, their passions provide the energy, and their purpose integrates both into a meaningful contribution.

The magic of life happens when your purpose becomes the expression of your deepest values and the celebration of your most fervent passions.

Conversely, consider someone whose values are knowledge, intellectual exploration, and social justice. Their passions might be research, writing, and advocacy. Their purpose could then be to conduct research on social inequalities, write compelling articles to raise awareness, and actively participate in advocacy groups to promote social change. Again, the integration of values and passions shapes a significant purpose, providing direction and fulfillment.

The process of connecting your purpose to your values and passions isn't always straightforward. It requires introspection, self-awareness, and a willingness to explore different avenues. Begin by listing your top five values. Ask yourself: What principles truly matter to you? What kind of world do you aspire to live in? What qualities do you admire most in others and in yourself? Next, identify your top three passions. What activities bring you joy and leave you feeling energized and engaged? What are you naturally curious about? What skills do you possess, or would love to develop, that could be applied to make a positive impact?

Once you have clearly identified your values and passions, look for points of convergence. Where do these elements overlap? What activities could you engage in that both align with your values and ignite your passions? This intersection is where your purpose begins to take shape. Don't be afraid to brainstorm freely; explore seemingly unrelated ideas, as unexpected connections may emerge. Write down all possibilities, even those that seem far-fetched at first. The act of writing itself can help clarify your thoughts and identify potential pathways.

The journey of discovering your purpose is often iterative, a process of refinement and growth. Your purpose may evolve over time as your values shift and new passions emerge. Life's experiences shape and reshape us, refining our understanding of ourselves and the world around us. This is not a failure; it's a sign of growth and adaptation. What resonates profoundly at one stage of life might feel less relevant at another, and that's perfectly acceptable. The beauty of this process lies in its ongoing evolution, mirroring the ever-changing tapestry of life itself.

It is very important to acknowledge that external factors can sometimes influence our perception of purpose. Societal expectations, familial pressures, and financial constraints can all impact our choices. However, a truly meaningful purpose must resonate deeply within; it cannot be dictated entirely by external forces. While considering external realities is essential for practical application, the core of your purpose should be rooted in your authentic values and passions. Don't allow external pressures to overshadow your inner compass. The alignment between your inner world and your outer actions is essential for long-term fulfillment.

To solidify this connection, create a visual representation of your values, passions, and emerging purpose. A mind map, a collage, or even a simple list can be a powerful tool for clarifying your thoughts and visualizing the interconnectedness of these elements. Visual aids can help reveal patterns and connections you might otherwise overlook. This visual representation can serve as a constant reminder of your purpose, a source of motivation during challenging times.

Don't settle for a life void of purpose. Let your values and passions be the architects of a life that ignites your soul and inspires the world.

Never forget to embrace the process of self-discovery, the exploration, the questioning, and even the occasional uncertainty. There will be moments of doubt, and that's perfectly normal. It's through these experiences, through the ebb and flow of life's challenges, that we deepen our understanding of ourselves and our purpose. Celebrate the small victories along the way, acknowledge the lessons learned from setbacks, and maintain a spirit of continuous learning and growth. Your purpose is an evolving story, reflecting the ever-changing narrative of your unique life. Embrace the journey, for within it lies the path to a life lived with authenticity, meaning, and profound fulfillment. This is not a race to the finish line; it's a life-long exploration, a continual refinement of your understanding of yourself and your place in the world.

PURPOSE AS A GUIDING STAR

Purpose acts as a compass, guiding us through the labyrinth of life's choices. Without a clear sense of purpose, we drift, easily swayed by external pressures and fleeting desires. We become reactive rather than proactive, letting circumstances dictate our path instead of consciously choosing our direction. Think of a ship at sea without a map or a compass — tossed about by the whims of the wind and waves, perpetually uncertain of its destination. That's how life can feel without a well-defined purpose.

But when we discover our purpose, we gain a sense of direction, a guiding star illuminating our path. It's not about finding a grand, singular purpose that dictates every moment of our lives.

Instead, it's about understanding the overarching theme, the underlying current that connects the various aspects of our lives – our work, our relationships, our personal pursuits. It provides a framework for making decisions, a filter through which we evaluate opportunities, and a source of intrinsic motivation that sustains us through challenges.

Imagine, for instance, someone deeply passionate about environmental conservation. Their purpose might be to protect and restore our planet's ecosystems. This doesn't mean every decision they make revolves solely around this purpose. They'll still need to manage their finances, maintain relationships, and attend to personal needs. However, their overarching purpose influences their choices. They might choose a career in environmental science, volunteer with a conservation organization, or advocate for environmentally friendly policies in their community. Even seemingly mundane tasks, such as recycling or choosing sustainable products, become aligned with their larger purpose. This alignment creates a powerful sense of meaning and fulfillment.

Contrast this with someone lacking a clear sense of purpose. They might feel lost, unfulfilled, and perpetually searching for something more. Their choices become fragmented, lacking a unifying theme. They may jump from job to job, relationship to relationship, without a sense of progress or direction. They feel pulled in various directions by external pressures – societal expectations, peer influence, the pursuit of material wealth – instead of being guided by an inner compass. This leads to a sense of dissatisfaction, a nagging feeling that something is missing.

Defining your purpose isn't about finding a pre-ordained destiny. It's an ongoing process of self-discovery, a continuous refinement of understanding based on your evolving values, passions, and experiences. It requires introspection, honest self-assessment, and a willingness to explore different avenues. It's a journey, not a destination, and it's perfectly acceptable – even expected – to have your understanding of purpose shift and evolve as you grow and learn.

One valuable approach is to identify areas where you consistently find yourself energized and engaged. What activities make you lose track of time? What tasks do you find yourself eagerly anticipating, even when facing challenges? These are often strong indicators of underlying passions, potential pathways towards your purpose. These passions are not always glamorous or obvious. They could be as simple as tending a garden, volunteering at a local animal shelter, or mastering a particular skill. But it is in these seemingly mundane actions that we often uncover profound connections to our true selves and our purpose.

In a world of fleeting trends, your purpose is the steadfast North Star, anchoring you to your true direction and guiding you toward your destiny.

Another crucial aspect is aligning your purpose with your values. Your values represent your core beliefs, the principles that guide your actions. If your purpose contradicts your values, you'll experience internal conflict and a lack of authenticity. For example, if your value is honesty and your purported purpose is to accumulate wealth through unethical means, you'll inevitably encounter dissonance and dissatisfaction. Your values act as a moral compass, ensuring your purpose remains ethically sound and aligned with your integrity.

Setting meaningful goals is a powerful tool in bringing your purpose to life. Goals provide a tangible pathway to achieving your purpose. Instead of simply stating, "My purpose is to help others," a more effective approach would be to set concrete, achievable goals. For example, "I will volunteer at a homeless shelter for two hours a week," or, "I will start a fundraising campaign for a local charity." These goals provide a roadmap, breaking down the larger purpose into manageable steps, and creating a sense of progress and accomplishment along the way.

Don't let the noise of the world drown out the quiet brilliance of your purpose. Let it be the guiding star that leads you to your authentic self.

It's important to remember that setbacks and challenges are inevitable in this journey. Don't let setbacks derail your efforts. Instead, view them as opportunities for growth, learning experiences that refine your understanding of your purpose and strengthen your resolve. Reflect on your experiences, adapt your approach, and persevere. Remember that the path to purpose is rarely linear. It's full of twists, turns, and detours. Embracing these experiences – the unexpected challenges, the unforeseen opportunities – is part of the process.

Engaging in consistent self-reflection is crucial. Regularly take time to assess your progress, re-evaluate your goals, and ensure your actions align with your purpose and values. Journaling, meditation, or simply spending time in nature can be helpful tools for self-reflection. Ask yourself probing questions. How does my current path align with my values and purpose? What adjustments do I need to make? What obstacles do I need to overcome? What lessons have I learned from my experiences?

Remember the power of seeking guidance. Connect with mentors, coaches, or trusted friends who can provide support, insights, and accountability. Sharing your journey with others can be incredibly valuable. They can offer fresh perspectives, help you stay motivated, and provide encouragement during challenging times. Their support can make the journey less daunting and more rewarding.

The journey of discovering and living your purpose is deeply personal and unique to you. There's no one-size-fits-all answer. It's a process of continuous self-discovery, adaptation, and growth. Embrace the journey, celebrate your progress, and never stop questioning, learning, and evolving. The path to a life filled with meaning and fulfillment is a journey worth taking, a voyage that will lead you towards a life lived authentically, intentionally, and with a deep sense of purpose. This journey of self-discovery is not about reaching a final destination but about continually refining your understanding of yourself and your place in the world, embracing the challenges, and savoring the victories along the way. It's a lifetime of growth and learning, and it is within this continuous journey that you will find not only your purpose but also a deeper appreciation for the beauty and complexity of your own unique life. The process is as important as the outcome, for it is in the striving, in the learning, in the overcoming of obstacles that we truly discover who we are meant to be.

PURPOSE IN ACTION PRACTICAL APPLICATION

The previous chapter laid the groundwork, helping you unearth the seeds of your purpose. Now, the crucial next step is to nurture those seeds, to cultivate them into a thriving, vibrant force that shapes your life. This isn't about some grand, singular revelation, but rather a consistent, conscious integration of your purpose into the fabric of your daily existence. Think of it less as a destination and more as a journey, a continuous process of refinement and growth.

Let's begin with your work life. Many find their purpose intertwined with their profession, not necessarily in terms of a career title, but in the impact they make. If you're already in a fulfilling career, wonderful! But even then, consider how you can amplify your contribution. Can you mentor a junior colleague, share your expertise through workshops or presentations, or take on projects that align more closely with your core values? If your work currently feels devoid of purpose, don't despair. This isn't a call to quit your job impulsively, but rather a prompt to introspect. What aspects of your work, however small, resonate with your values? Can you find ways to enhance those aspects? Perhaps it's taking initiative on a project that allows you to use your creativity, or volunteering for tasks that leverage your problem-solving skills. Even small shifts can make a significant difference in how engaged and fulfilled you feel.

Consider the power of aligning your skills and passions with your purpose. Perhaps you're a skilled writer, but your current job involves data entry. Could you dedicate some evenings to freelance writing, gradually shifting towards a career that better reflects your purpose? Maybe you're a compassionate listener, and your purpose involves helping others. Could you volunteer at a local soup kitchen or offer support to a friend going through a difficult time? These actions, while seemingly small, are powerful affirmations of your values and a vital step towards living a more purposeful life. Don't underestimate the impact of small, consistent actions. These are the building blocks of a life aligned with your deepest self.

Moving beyond the professional sphere, let's consider your relationships. How can your purpose enhance your connections with loved ones? If your purpose involves nurturing creativity, perhaps you can initiate a family art project. If your purpose involves fostering community, maybe you can organize a neighborhood gathering. If your purpose involves personal growth, perhaps you can engage in shared learning experiences with friends or family. It's not about imposing your purpose on others, but about finding ways to integrate it into your interactions in a meaningful and authentic way. This might involve sharing your passions, supporting their endeavors, or simply engaging in activities that align with your shared values.

The beauty of defining your purpose lies in its potential to enrich all aspects of your life. It's not just about a grand career or a life-altering decision; it's about the daily choices you make, the small acts of kindness you perform, and the subtle shifts in perspective you adopt. It's about how you spend your time, who you choose to spend it with, and what kind of energy you bring to each interaction. It's about recognizing the power of your choices and making them consciously, intentionally, and authentically. This is about cultivating a deeper sense of presence in your day-to-day life, finding joy in the small moments, and actively seeking opportunities to express your purpose.

Personal pursuits are another crucial area where your purpose can flourish. This might involve hobbies, creative endeavors, volunteering, or simply engaging in activities that bring you joy and fulfillment. If your purpose involves fostering connection, perhaps you join a book club or volunteer at a local animal shelter. If your purpose involves physical and mental well-being, maybe you dedicate time to yoga, meditation, or spending time in nature. These activities are not just distractions or escapes; they are powerful expressions of your values and a vital component of a life lived with purpose. They provide opportunities for self-care, personal growth, and the cultivation of inner peace.

The key to successfully integrating your purpose into your daily life lies in consistent action. This isn't a one-time event but a continuous process of refining your understanding of your purpose and adapting your actions to align with it. There will be days when you feel strongly connected to your purpose, and there will be days when you struggle. This is perfectly normal. The important thing is to maintain a consistent effort, to keep moving forward, even when progress feels slow. Small steps, consistently taken, eventually lead to significant change. Celebrate your successes, learn from your setbacks, and never stop striving towards a life lived with intention and meaning.

One of the most effective ways to keep your purpose at the forefront of your mind is to create visual reminders. This might involve writing down your purpose statement and placing it somewhere prominent, such as your desk or bathroom mirror. You could also create a vision board filled with images and words that represent your purpose. These visual reminders serve as powerful affirmations, helping to keep your focus and motivation strong. They serve as tangible symbols of your aspirations and a constant reminder of the life you're striving to create. It's about bringing your aspirations into your everyday consciousness, making them a part of your everyday landscape.

When you feel lost in the vastness of life, look inward and find your purpose, the guiding star that will lead you home to yourself.

Write about your experiences, your challenges, and your triumphs. Reflect on how your actions align with your purpose, and identify areas where you can make adjustments. This practice of self-reflection is invaluable in fostering self-awareness and sustaining momentum. It's a form of self-coaching, helping you to maintain focus and navigate the inevitable challenges that will arise along the way.

Remember, your purpose isn't static. It's a living, evolving entity that will change and adapt as you grow and learn. Be open to this evolution. Embrace the changes, and allow your purpose to guide you towards new experiences and opportunities. This isn't a fixed destination, but a dynamic journey of continuous self-discovery. The process itself is as important as the destination, for it's in the striving, the adapting, and the learning that you truly come to understand yourself and your place in the world.

Don't be afraid to experiment and try new things. Step outside your comfort zone and explore different avenues. You might discover unexpected passions and talents, leading you towards even greater fulfillment. This journey is about exploration, discovery, and embracing the uncertainty of the unknown. The more you actively engage with your purpose, the more clearly it will reveal itself to you.

Finally, remember it's normal to experience setbacks and periods of uncertainty. Don't let these moments derail your progress. Instead, view them as opportunities for growth and learning. Embrace your imperfections, celebrate your strengths, and never stop believing in your ability to create a life filled with meaning and purpose. This is a journey of self-discovery, and it's a journey worth taking, a voyage that will ultimately lead you to a life lived authentically, intentionally, and with a deep sense of purpose. Embrace the journey, celebrate your progress, and never stop evolving.

THE EVOLVING NATURE OF PURPOSE

The understanding of our purpose isn't a singular, lightning-bolt revelation; it's more like a gentle sunrise, slowly illuminating the landscape of our lives. It dawns gradually, revealing new facets and dimensions as we navigate the complexities of existence. To believe our purpose is fixed, and unchanging, is to limit ourselves, to stifle the very growth and evolution that defines the human experience. Imagine a tree, its roots firmly planted in the earth, yet its branches reaching ever higher towards the sun, constantly adapting to the changing seasons, the shifting winds. Our purpose is much the same: a dynamic entity, ever-responding to the environment, to our experiences, to our evolving selves.

One of the most significant factors influencing this evolution is personal growth. As we learn, we change. We acquire new skills, encounter fresh perspectives, and confront challenges that reshape our understanding of ourselves and the world around us. This process inevitably alters our sense of purpose. What deeply resonated with us at twenty may feel less relevant at forty, and that's perfectly natural. Our priorities shift, our passions deepen, and our capabilities expand. Consider the individual who initially envisioned their purpose as climbing the corporate ladder, driven by ambition and a desire for financial security. Years later, they may find that their definition of success has evolved. Perhaps they now prioritize work-life balance, community engagement, or the pursuit of a creative passion they previously neglected. This is not a betrayal of their initial purpose; it's an evolution, a refinement based on the lessons learned and the experiences gained.

Another powerful force shaping our evolving purpose is our relationships. The people we encounter, the bonds we forge, and the connections we nurture profoundly influence our direction in life. A supportive mentor can inspire us to pursue goals we hadn't previously considered. A loving partner can challenge us to grow in unexpected ways. A close friend might illuminate a hidden talent or passion we hadn't realized we possessed. These interactions shape our perspectives, expanding our horizons and enriching our sense of purpose. Think about a young artist struggling to find their voice, feeling lost and alone in their creative journey. Then, imagine them connecting with a community of fellow artists, sharing their work, receiving encouragement, and finding inspiration in the diverse talents of others. This community becomes an integral part of their purpose, providing support, feedback, and a shared sense of belonging. Their initial solitary pursuit transforms into a collaborative endeavor, a validation of the dynamic nature of purpose.

Embrace the evolving nature of your purpose, for it is in the dance of change that you discover the deeper rhythms of your soul's calling.

Life's inevitable challenges also play a crucial role in shaping our purpose. It's often during times of adversity that we discover our deepest strengths and most profound values. A debilitating illness might lead us to re-evaluate our priorities, focusing on health and well-being in ways we never thought possible. The loss of a loved one can inspire us to dedicate our lives to a cause that honors their memory. A career setback might lead us down an unexpected path that ultimately proves more fulfilling. These experiences, though painful at times, often serve as catalysts for personal growth and a profound reshaping of our purpose. Consider the entrepreneur who faced a devastating business failure. Rather than succumbing to despair, they leveraged their experience, using the lessons learned to create a more sustainable and socially responsible enterprise. Their initial purpose — business success — evolved into a purpose-driven by both profit and positive impact.

It's vital to understand that this continuous evolution isn't a sign of weakness or indecisiveness; it's an attestation to our resilience and capacity for growth. Embracing this dynamic nature of purpose requires a willingness to be open to change, to adapt to new circumstances, and to trust in the unfolding of our lives. It necessitates a commitment to ongoing self-reflection, a willingness to honestly assess our values and priorities, and the courage to adjust our course as needed. The path to a fulfilling life isn't a straight line; it's a winding road, filled with unexpected turns and detours. It is precisely these unexpected turns, these moments of uncertainty, that often lead us to a deeper understanding of our true purpose.

Don't cling to a static definition of purpose.
Allow it to bloom and transform, revealing the infinite layers of your potential.

Recognizing the evolving nature of our purpose frees us from the pressure of finding the "one true calling." There is no single, definitive answer; instead, our purpose may manifest in many different forms throughout our lives. It's a mosaic, composed of various facets that shift and change over time, each contributing to the larger picture. Consider someone who begins their career in finance, later shifting to environmental advocacy, then eventually finding fulfillment in teaching young children. Each of these seemingly disparate paths contributes to a holistic purpose – a commitment to impacting the world positively, be it through financial stability, environmental conservation, or inspiring future generations.

The key is to remain open to the possibilities that unfold before us, to embrace change as an opportunity for growth, and to constantly reflect on our values and aspirations. Regularly asking ourselves questions such as, "What truly matters to me?", "What brings me joy and fulfillment?", "How can I use my talents and skills to make a positive impact?" will help us to stay aligned with our evolving purpose. This isn't just about career paths; it encompasses our relationships, our hobbies, our contributions to society – everything that constitutes our unique and ever-shifting life story. It's about creating a life that is authentically ours, a life that reflects our deepest values and aspirations at every stage of our journey.

Therefore, the process of defining your purpose is not a destination; it's a continuous journey of self-discovery, adaptation, and refinement. It's about embracing the fluidity of life, allowing your purpose to evolve and adapt as you grow and learn. It is about recognizing that the experiences, relationships, and challenges you encounter are not obstacles, but rather valuable lessons that guide you towards a deeper, more authentic understanding of who you are and what you are meant to contribute to the world. Don't be afraid to revise your purpose, to adjust your direction, to let your life's narrative unfold organically. This continuous evolution is not a sign of failure; it's a confirmation of your growth, resilience, and capacity for ongoing transformation. The beauty lies in the journey itself, the constant striving, the ongoing quest for deeper meaning and fulfillment. This journey, this continuous exploration, is the essence of a life lived authentically and with purpose.

Consider the concept of "ikigai," a Japanese term often translated as "a reason for being." Ikigai isn't necessarily a singular, static purpose but rather the intersection of what you love, what you're good at, what the world needs, and what you can be paid for. As your skills grow, your passions shift, and the world's needs change, your ikigai will naturally evolve. It's not a fixed point but a dynamic space where these four elements continuously interact and reshape each other. This illustrates the evolving nature of purpose perfectly; it's a dynamic interplay, constantly adjusting and refining itself in response to internal growth and external shifts. It's not about finding the ultimate, unchanging purpose, but about cultivating a life where these four elements continually inform and shape one another, creating a sense of meaning and fulfillment along the way.

Ultimately, the evolving nature of purpose allows for resilience, adaptability, and continuous growth. It permits us to embrace change, learn from setbacks, and continuously redefine our goals and aspirations to better align with our current selves. It releases us from the pressure of a rigidly defined path, freeing us to explore new horizons and experience the enriching diversity of life's many offerings. It invites us to see our lives as a continuous work in progress, a profound substance merged from experiences, relationships, and challenges, all contributing to a richer, more meaningful, and ultimately more fulfilling existence. This fluid approach to purpose enables us to remain flexible and responsive to the ever-changing landscape of life, ensuring our journey is not only purposeful but deeply satisfying and genuinely our own.

Don't fear the shifting sands of your purpose. Embrace the evolution, for it is in the transformation that you discover your true resilience.

LIFE OF PURPOSE
ACTIONABLE STRATEGIES
SETTING MEANINGFUL GOALS

Setting meaningful goals isn't about ticking off items on a to-do list; it's about aligning your actions with the deeper purpose you've uncovered. It's about crafting a life that resonates with your authentic self, not one dictated by external pressures or fleeting desires. This process requires introspection, clarity, and a willingness to embrace both ambition and vulnerability. Remember, the journey of self-discovery is ongoing, and your goals should reflect that continuous evolution.

The first step in setting meaningful goals is to revisit your core values and passions. What truly matters to you? What ignites your inner fire? These aren't abstract concepts; they should be the foundation upon which you build your aspirations. If your values include creativity and connection, your goals might involve starting a blog, joining a writing group, or volunteering for a cause you care about. If your passion lies in learning, your goals might include taking online courses, attending workshops, or pursuing further education.

Avoid the trap of setting goals solely based on external validation. Society often bombards us with messages about what constitutes "success"—a high-paying job, a luxurious lifestyle, a large social media following. These external metrics can be alluring, but they rarely align with our deepest sense of purpose. Instead, focus on goals that nurture your inner growth, contribute to your well-being, and allow you to live in accordance with your values.

When crafting your goals, use the SMART framework as a guide: Specific, Measurable, Achievable, Relevant, and Time-bound. A vague goal like "be healthier" is far less effective than a specific goal like "exercise for 30 minutes three times a week for the next three months." Specificity provides clarity and direction, making it easier to track your progress and stay motivated. Measurability allows you to objectively assess your achievements and celebrate your successes, fostering a sense of accomplishment. Achievability ensures that your goals are challenging yet attainable, preventing discouragement and fostering perseverance. Relevance ensures that your goals align with your overall purpose and values, reinforcing your commitment. Finally, a time-bound aspect provides a sense of urgency and focus, preventing procrastination and ensuring timely completion.

Let's illustrate this with some examples. Imagine you've identified a deep-seated passion for helping others and a core value of compassion. Using the SMART framework, you could set the following goals:

SPECIFIC: Volunteer at a local homeless shelter for two hours every Saturday for the next six months.

MEASURABLE: Track the number of hours volunteered each month and the impact made (e.g., number of meals served, people assisted).

ACHIEVABLE: Start with two hours per week, gradually increasing the commitment if desired.

RELEVANT: This aligns directly with your passion for helping others and your value of compassion.

TIME-BOUND: The six-month timeframe provides a clear deadline and a sense of urgency.

Or perhaps you've discovered a passion for writing and a value of self-expression. Using the SMART framework, you could set the following goals:

SPECIFIC: Write and submit a short story to a literary magazine each month for the next year.

MEASURABLE: Track the number of submissions and the responses received.

ACHIEVABLE: Set aside dedicated writing time each week to ensure consistent progress.

RELEVANT: This aligns directly with your passion for writing and your value of self-expression.

Time-bound: The one-year timeframe provides a clear deadline and a sense of urgency.

Remember that your goals should be challenging but not overwhelming. Setting excessively ambitious goals can lead to burnout and discouragement. Start small, focus on consistent progress, and gradually increase the difficulty as you gain confidence and experience.

Once you've established your goals, create a supportive environment around you. This means surrounding yourself with individuals who understand and encourage your aspirations. It might involve seeking mentors who have already achieved what you hope to achieve, or joining communities of like-minded individuals who share your values and passions. This network provides invaluable support, guidance, and accountability, helping you stay motivated and overcome challenges.

The path to a purposeful life isn't always smooth. There will be setbacks, obstacles, and moments of self-doubt. But these challenges are inevitable parts of the journey, and learning to navigate them is crucial. Develop resilience by focusing on your "why." When faced with adversity, remind yourself of the deeper purpose driving your actions, and re-affirm your commitment to your goals.

Don't underestimate the power of celebrating milestones and progress. Acknowledge your achievements, no matter how small. This isn't about ego; it's about reinforcing positive self-perception and building momentum. Regularly review your goals, acknowledge progress made, and adjust your approach as needed. This process helps to stay motivated and prevents discouragement. Remember that self-compassion is key. Forgive yourself for setbacks, learn from your mistakes, and continue to move forward.

Recognize that your journey of self-discovery is a lifelong process. Your values, passions, and purpose may evolve over time as you grow and learn. Therefore, regularly revisit and revise your goals, ensuring that they remain aligned with your evolving sense of self. This ongoing process of reflection and adaptation is crucial for maintaining a meaningful and fulfilling life. Embrace the continuous growth and the ever-evolving nature of your aspirations. The key is to remain flexible, adaptable, and committed to the ongoing process of self-discovery and goal achievement. Your journey is unique, and your goals should reflect that uniqueness.

Remember, setting meaningful goals isn't about achieving a specific outcome; it's about the journey itself, about the continuous process of growth, learning, and self-discovery. It's about aligning your actions with your authentic self, and creating a life that resonates with your values and passions. Through consistent effort, self-compassion, and a willingness to embrace the unexpected, you can build a life of purpose, fulfillment, and lasting satisfaction. Embrace the challenge, trust the process, and celebrate your journey.

SUPPORTIVE ENVIRONMENT

The journey towards a life of purpose isn't a solitary trek across a barren landscape. It's a shared expedition, a collaborative climb up a mountain, where the support of others becomes as crucial as the strength in your own legs. Having laid the groundwork of self-discovery and meaningful goal-setting, we now turn to the crucial element of building a supportive environment – a network of individuals who understand your aspirations, champion your growth, and offer a helping hand when the path gets steep.

This isn't about superficial connections or fleeting friendships. This is about cultivating deep, meaningful relationships with people who genuinely care about your well-being and progress. These relationships can come in various forms – family members who offer unconditional love and encouragement, friends who understand your struggles and celebrate your triumphs, and mentors who guide you with their wisdom and experience.

Let's start with family. Family dynamics can be complex, often fraught with challenges and unresolved issues. But within those complexities lies a potential wellspring of support. Think back to your family history – perhaps a grandparent who instilled in you a love for learning, a parent who showed you the value of hard work, or a sibling who challenged you to push your boundaries. These influences, often subtle, shaped your character and laid the foundation for your aspirations. Rekindling those positive connections, or addressing unresolved conflicts, can be transformative. A family member's unwavering belief in you can provide the emotional anchor you need during challenging times. Honest communication, even about difficult topics, can strengthen these bonds and unlock a vital source of support.

Next, let's consider friends. True friends are more than just casual acquaintances. They are the individuals who understand your deepest vulnerabilities, celebrate your successes, and offer comfort during setbacks. They're the ones who don't shy away from difficult conversations, who offer honest feedback, and who challenge you to grow beyond your comfort zone. If you're struggling to find friends who align with your values and aspirations, consider actively seeking out communities or groups that share your interests. Volunteering, joining a book club, participating in workshops, or engaging in online forums can help you connect with like-minded individuals. Remember, building authentic friendships takes time and effort. Be patient, be genuine, and be willing to invest in the relationships that truly matter.

Mentorship plays a particularly critical role in navigating the path to purpose. A mentor can be anyone who has achieved something you aspire to achieve, who possesses wisdom and experience you can learn from, and who is willing to guide you along the way. This doesn't necessarily mean finding a formal mentor; it could be a colleague, a teacher, a family friend, or even someone you've connected with online. The key is to find someone you admire and respect, whose values align with your own, and who is willing to invest time in your growth.

Identifying potential mentors requires introspection. Who are the people you admire? Whose accomplishments inspire you? Who has overcome obstacles you're currently facing? Once you have a few candidates in mind, reach out to them. Don't be afraid to express your admiration and to ask for guidance. Prepare some specific questions to show that you're thoughtful and prepared. A successful mentorship relationship is built on mutual respect, open communication, and a willingness to learn. The mentor-mentee dynamic should feel collaborative, not hierarchical. Consider it a two-way street—your insights and perspectives can be valuable to your mentor as well.

BUT WHAT IF YOUR EXISTING RELATIONSHIPS ARE NOT SUPPORTIVE?

What if your family is critical, your friends are dismissive, and you feel alone in your quest for purpose? This is where self-compassion and assertive communication become essential.

SELF-COMPASSION means treating yourself with the same kindness and understanding you would offer a dear friend facing similar challenges. Recognize that everyone experiences setbacks, and that it's okay to feel vulnerable, frustrated, or even discouraged at times. Avoid self-criticism and negative self-talk. Instead, approach your challenges with empathy and self-acceptance.

ASSERTIVE COMMUNICATION is equally crucial. It's about expressing your needs and boundaries respectfully, even when it's difficult. If you're in a relationship that's consistently draining or negative, you may need to set boundaries or even distance yourself. This doesn't mean you have to sever all ties; it means protecting your energy and focusing on the relationships that nourish you. Learn to say "no" to commitments that don't align with your priorities, and communicate your needs clearly and directly.

Building a supportive environment isn't a passive activity. It's a conscious choice, an intentional effort to cultivate relationships that fuel your journey towards purpose. It involves identifying the individuals who can offer you support, fostering those relationships, and setting healthy boundaries with those who may not be aligned with your aspirations. Remember, the quality of your relationships significantly impacts your overall well-being and your ability to achieve your goals. Invest time and energy in building strong, supportive connections, and you'll find that the path toward purpose becomes significantly smoother and more fulfilling.

Beyond the immediate circle of family, friends, and mentors, consider the broader community. Engaging with like-minded individuals, even casually, can provide a sense of belonging and shared purpose. Joining groups related to your interests, volunteering your time, or participating in community events can expand your network and connect you with individuals who share your values. This sense of community can provide invaluable emotional support and a feeling of connection that's crucial for navigating the challenges of life. It's a reminder that you're not alone in your journey.

Think about the power of shared experiences. Whether it's a challenging hike with friends, a collaborative work project with colleagues, or a volunteer effort with your community, these shared experiences foster deeper bonds and a sense of collective purpose. These moments build resilience, enhance communication, and create a feeling of belonging that strengthens your resolve in pursuing your goals.

Furthermore, online communities can play an unexpectedly significant role in building a supportive environment. Numerous online forums, social media groups, and professional networks are dedicated to specific interests, hobbies, or professions. Connecting with individuals who share your passions can provide a sense of camaraderie, inspiration, and access to a wider range of perspectives. This is especially valuable for individuals who might not have access to supportive communities in their immediate geographical location. However, remember to be mindful of online interactions, practicing responsible digital citizenship and prioritizing genuine connections over superficial ones.

Finally, consider the importance of self-care in nurturing your supportive environment. You can't pour from an empty cup. Prioritizing your physical, emotional, and mental well-being is essential to maintain healthy relationships and effectively navigate challenges. This might involve regular exercise, mindful meditation, healthy eating habits, sufficient sleep, or engaging in hobbies that bring you joy. By taking care of yourself, you become better equipped to offer support to others and to effectively navigate the inevitable ups and downs of your journey towards purpose. Remember that self-care isn't selfish;

it's a necessary investment in your overall well-being and your ability to contribute meaningfully to your supportive network. Building a life of purpose is a marathon, not a sprint, and self-care fuels your endurance.

MANAGING CHALLENGES AND SEATBACKS

The journey towards a life of purpose, as we've discussed, is rarely a smooth, upward trajectory. It's more akin to navigating a winding mountain road: exhilarating climbs interspersed with unexpected hairpin turns, steep descents, and the occasional roadblock. The key to reaching your summit isn't avoiding these challenges, but learning to navigate them with grace, resilience, and a renewed sense of purpose. This involves developing strategies not just for anticipating obstacles, but for effectively managing setbacks when they inevitably occur.

One of the most crucial skills in this process is cultivating a mindset of resilience. Resilience isn't about denying the pain or difficulty of a setback; rather, it's about your ability to bounce back from adversity, to learn from your failures, and to emerge stronger and more determined than before. Imagine a willow tree bending in a strong wind – it doesn't break because it's flexible, it adapts. We can cultivate that same flexibility in our own lives.

This involves developing a realistic perspective on setbacks. Often, we tend to catastrophize our mistakes, viewing them as insurmountable obstacles rather than learning opportunities. Instead of dwelling on "what if" scenarios and beating yourself up over past decisions, try reframing your perspective. Ask yourself: "What can I learn from this experience? What steps can I take to prevent this from happening again? How can I use this knowledge to propel me forward?" This shift in perspective transforms setbacks from debilitating events into valuable steppingstones on your journey.

Building a strong support system is also paramount. Remember that chapter on nurturing your network? Leaning on trusted friends, family, mentors, or even a therapist can provide the emotional support and practical guidance needed to weather difficult times. These individuals can offer a fresh perspective, help you problem-solve, and remind you of your strengths when you're feeling overwhelmed. Don't be afraid to reach out; vulnerability is a sign of strength, not weakness. Sharing your struggles with others is a sign of courage and allows you to receive the support you need to rebuild and regain momentum.

Another critical component of managing challenges is the ability to effectively manage stress. Chronic stress can be debilitating, hindering your progress and impacting your overall well-being. Therefore, incorporating stress-management techniques into your daily routine is essential. This might involve practicing mindfulness meditation, engaging in regular physical activity, spending time in nature, listening to calming music, or pursuing hobbies that bring you joy. Find what works best for you and make it a non-negotiable part of your self-care routine. Remember, self-care isn't selfish; it's an investment in your ability to navigate challenges effectively.

Furthermore, developing a robust problem-solving framework is essential. When confronted with a setback, it's easy to become paralyzed by fear and uncertainty. However, by approaching challenges with a structured approach, you can regain control and move forward with purpose. Begin by clearly defining the problem. What exactly is the obstacle you're facing? Then, brainstorm potential solutions. Don't censor your ideas at this stage; the goal is to generate a wide range of possibilities. Next, evaluate the feasibility and potential consequences of each solution. This involves considering the resources required, the potential risks, and the likelihood of success. Finally, choose the most promising solution and implement it, ensuring you have a plan for monitoring progress and making adjustments as needed.

Beyond practical strategies, cultivating emotional intelligence is vital. This involves understanding and managing your own emotions, as well as recognizing and empathizing with the feelings of others. Emotional intelligence enables you to navigate difficult conversations, resolve conflicts constructively, and build stronger relationships — all crucial for navigating the inevitable challenges on your path to purpose. Self-awareness is the cornerstone of emotional intelligence. Pay attention to your emotional responses to setbacks. Are you prone to anger, frustration, or despair? Understanding these patterns allows you to develop coping mechanisms to regulate your emotions and respond more effectively to challenges.

Finally, remember to celebrate your small victories along the way. The journey towards a life of purpose is not a sprint; it's a marathon. There will be many small wins, moments of progress, and signs of your growth. Acknowledge and celebrate these milestones, no matter how insignificant they may seem. These small victories provide the motivation and encouragement needed to persevere through the inevitable challenges. Keep a journal to document your progress, noting both your successes and the lessons learned from setbacks. This creates a tangible record of your journey, reminding you of how far you've come and bolstering your confidence to continue moving forward.

Let's consider some specific examples. Imagine you're an entrepreneur launching a new business. You've poured your heart and soul into this venture, only to see initial sales fall far short of your projections. Instead of giving up, a resilient approach involves analyzing the reasons behind the low sales — is it poor marketing, pricing issues, or a lack of awareness? This analytical process allows you to adapt your strategy, perhaps refining your marketing campaign, adjusting your pricing model, or exploring new avenues for reaching your target market. This process of learning and adapting is the essence of resilience.

Or perhaps you're pursuing a career change, facing rejection after rejection from potential employers. Instead of internalizing these setbacks as personal failures, you can reframe them as opportunities to refine your resume, improve your interviewing skills, and network more effectively. You can seek feedback from those who interviewed you, learning from their perspectives and improving your candidacy. Each rejection becomes a lesson, bringing you closer to your ultimate goal.

The path to a purposeful life is rarely linear. It's characterized by twists, turns, and setbacks. The key to success lies in embracing these challenges as opportunities for growth, developing resilience, building a strong support network, and honing your problem-solving skills. Remember, it's not about avoiding hardship but about developing the inner strength and wisdom to navigate it with grace and determination. By cultivating these skills, you equip yourself not only to manage setbacks but to thrive in the face of adversity, ultimately reaching your desired destination with a deeper understanding of yourself and your purpose. The journey, with its inherent challenges, becomes an integral part of the destination itself, shaping your character and enriching your experience. Embrace the process, learn from every stumble, and celebrate every milestone – that's the true essence of building a life of purpose.

CELEBRATING MILESTONES AND PROGRESS

We often get so caught up in the striving, in the relentless pursuit of our goals, that we forget to pause, to breathe, to simply acknowledge how far we've come. The journey toward a life of purpose is a marathon, not a sprint, and neglecting to celebrate the smaller victories along the way can lead to burnout, discouragement, and ultimately, a derailment of our ambitions. Think of it like climbing a mountain; the summit is the ultimate goal, but the breathtaking views from each conquered plateau, and the sense of accomplishment after navigating a particularly treacherous slope, these are the milestones that fuel our perseverance and keep our spirits high.

We're frequently far more critical of ourselves than we would ever be of a friend struggling with a similar challenge. Imagine a friend striving towards the same goal; wouldn't you celebrate their small wins, offer encouragement during setbacks, and remind them of their strengths? Extend that same kindness and understanding to yourself. Acknowledge that progress isn't always linear. There will be days, weeks, even months, when you feel like you're moving backward. These are simply moments of recalibration, opportunities to reassess your strategy, and to reinforce your commitment to your ultimate vision.

Celebrating milestones isn't about vanity or self-aggrandizement; it's about actively reinforcing positive behaviors and cultivating a mindset of gratitude.

When we acknowledge our accomplishments, no matter how small, we reinforce the neural pathways associated with those successes. This creates a positive feedback loop, making it more likely that we will repeat those behaviors in the future. It's like giving your brain a reward for good work, strengthening its commitment to the process. This positive reinforcement is crucial for maintaining momentum, especially during challenging periods.

How can we effectively celebrate our progress? The answer is personal and unique to each individual. Some might find solace in quiet reflection, journaling their achievements and expressing gratitude for the lessons learned along the way. Others might prefer sharing their successes with loved ones, drawing strength and encouragement from their support system. Some might choose a more tangible celebration, rewarding themselves with a small treat or a special experience that aligns with their values. The key is to find a method that genuinely resonates with you, a method that feels authentic and meaningful, and not something imposed by external pressures or societal expectations.

Think about what truly inspires you. Is it the feeling of accomplishment after completing a challenging task? The joy of witnessing tangible progress towards a long-term goal? The satisfaction of helping others along the way? Tap into these intrinsic motivators when designing your celebration rituals. If you've successfully completed a challenging project at work, perhaps a relaxing evening with a good book and a warm bath will be the perfect reward. If you've conquered a particularly stubborn fear, a celebratory dinner with friends might be a fitting way to commemorate your courage and resilience. The crucial element is that the celebration feels meaningful and aligns with your personal values.

This process of self-acknowledgment extends beyond grand achievements. We must also learn to appreciate the small, everyday victories that often go unnoticed. The consistent effort to maintain a healthy lifestyle, the commitment to a daily meditation practice, the act of kindness extended to a stranger—these seemingly insignificant actions accumulate over time, contributing significantly to a life of purpose and fulfillment. When we pay attention to these incremental victories, we cultivate a deeper sense of self-awareness and self-efficacy, believing in our ability to create the life we desire.

Remember, the journey toward a life of purpose is not a solo expedition. Connecting with others who share similar goals, or who have already achieved what you aspire to, can provide invaluable insight, guidance, and support. Joining a community, whether online or in person, allows you to share experiences, learn from others' mistakes, and celebrate each other's successes. This shared journey fosters a sense of belonging and collective accomplishment, strengthening your resolve and bolstering your belief in the possibility of realizing your dreams.

Moreover, celebrating milestones is not just about looking back and acknowledging what has been achieved; it's also about using those accomplishments as springboards for future growth. Analyzing your past successes can reveal patterns and strategies that contributed to your achievements. What worked well? What challenges did you overcome? What lessons did you learn? Reflecting on these aspects can help you refine your approach, identify areas for improvement, and set more ambitious goals for the future.

Finally, remember that celebrating milestones isn't a selfish act; it's an essential part of self-care and sustainability. Ignoring our achievements can lead to feelings of inadequacy and discouragement, hindering our progress. By consciously acknowledging and celebrating our accomplishments, we recharge our emotional batteries, reinforcing our motivation and commitment to our purpose. This is not a luxury; it's a necessity for sustained growth and a fulfilling life. It is an act of self-love and self-respect, recognizing the effort, dedication, and resilience required to reach even the smallest of milestones on your journey. Embrace the celebration; you've earned it. And remember, each milestone reached is a step closer to the life you were meant to live. Embrace the journey, savor the moments, and celebrate your progress. You are doing remarkably well.

CONTINUOUS GROWTH AND SELF REFLECTION

Let self-reflection be the mirror that reveals your inner landscape, and continuous growth the gentle hand that shapes it into a masterpiece of being!

The journey towards a life of purpose isn't a destination; it's a continuous evolution. Reaching a significant milestone, achieving a long-held goal, doesn't mark the end of the path, but rather a transition to the next phase of our unfolding selves. This is where the crucial element of continuous growth and self-reflection comes into play. It's about embracing the ongoing process of learning, adapting, and refining our understanding of ourselves and our place in the world. Think of it as a spiral, not a straight line, each loop building upon the previous one, expanding our awareness and deepening our connection to our authentic selves.

The human experience is inherently dynamic. We are not static beings; we are constantly changing, evolving, and learning. What resonated deeply with us five years ago might feel irrelevant or even limiting today. Our values, priorities, and aspirations shift and morph as we navigate life's myriad experiences. To remain stagnant is to deny our very nature, to stifle our potential for growth and fulfillment. Continuous self-reflection provides the compass to guide us through this ever-changing landscape, ensuring we remain true to our evolving sense of self.

This reflection isn't merely about analyzing past successes and failures; it's about actively engaging with the present moment, paying attention to our emotional and mental states, and identifying patterns that illuminate our strengths, weaknesses, and blind spots. Journaling, meditation, and mindful introspection are valuable tools in this process. Regularly asking ourselves probing questions – "What am I learning from this experience?", "What are my current values and how are they guiding my actions?", "Am I truly aligned with my purpose, or have my priorities shifted?" – can provide profound insights into our inner world.

Continuous growth is the art of becoming, a lifelong journey of self-discovery fueled by the honest and compassionate gaze of self-reflection.

The act of self-reflection should be approached with kindness and compassion. It's not about self-criticism or judgment, but about self-understanding. We all make mistakes; we all experience setbacks. These experiences, however painful they may be, are invaluable opportunities for growth. By examining them honestly, without self-recrimination, we can extract valuable lessons, identify areas for improvement, and develop greater resilience. Instead of dwelling on failures, focus on what you learned from them, what adjustments you can make, and how you can apply that knowledge to future endeavors.

Furthermore, continuous growth requires a willingness to adapt and change. Life throws curveballs; unexpected challenges arise, forcing us to reconsider our plans and adjust our strategies. Rigidity and inflexibility can hinder our progress, trapping us in a cycle of frustration and disappointment. Embracing adaptability means cultivating a flexible mindset, one that is open to new ideas, perspectives, and possibilities. It involves being willing to step outside our comfort zones, to embrace uncertainty, and to learn from our mistakes. Remember, it's not about abandoning our purpose but about refining and recalibrating our approach as we gather more knowledge and experience.

Consider the example of a budding entrepreneur launching a new business. Initially, their vision might be laser-focused on a specific product or service. However, as they gather market feedback, they realize that their initial assumptions were incorrect. Instead of stubbornly clinging to their original plan, a truly adaptable entrepreneur would embrace this feedback, modifying their product or service to better meet the needs of their target audience. This adaptability, fueled by continuous self-reflection and a willingness to learn, often proves to be the key to success.

Self-reflection is the still pond where you see the depths of your being, and continuous growth is the ripple that expands your understanding of yourself and the world.

Allow self-reflection to be the gentle guide that illuminates your path, and the continuous growth of your unwavering commitment to becoming the best version of yourself.

The process of self-reflection also involves actively seeking feedback from trusted sources. This doesn't mean seeking validation; rather, it's about gaining objective insights into our blind spots. We might be unaware of certain behaviors or patterns that hinder our progress. A supportive friend, family member, mentor, or therapist can offer valuable perspectives that broaden our understanding of ourselves. Listen to their feedback with an open mind, acknowledging their viewpoints, even if they challenge your own. The goal is to gain a more comprehensive picture of yourself, not to satisfy everyone's expectations.

Continuous growth also necessitates a commitment to lifelong learning. It's about cultivating a thirst for knowledge, embracing new experiences, and expanding our horizons. This can involve formal education, reading, attending workshops, engaging in conversations with people from diverse backgrounds, or traveling to new places. The opportunities for learning are limitless, and actively seeking them out demonstrates a commitment to personal development.

This commitment to lifelong learning should extend beyond professional development to encompass personal growth.

Explore new hobbies, take up a new skill, connect with nature, or simply spend time reflecting on your experiences. These activities nourish the soul, fostering creativity, resilience, and a deeper understanding of ourselves. Remember, continuous growth is not just about acquiring new knowledge; it's about expanding our perspectives, strengthening our resilience, and enriching our lives.

Another crucial aspect of continuous growth is the practice of self-compassion. This means treating ourselves with the same kindness and understanding that we would offer a close friend facing similar challenges. We often hold ourselves to impossibly high standards, harshly criticizing ourselves for mistakes and setbacks. This self-criticism can be debilitating, hindering our progress and fostering feelings of inadequacy. Self-compassion involves acknowledging our imperfections, accepting our vulnerabilities, and recognizing that we are all works in progress. It's about giving ourselves permission to make mistakes, to learn from them, and to move forward with renewed determination.

Moreover, continuous growth is intrinsically linked to self-care. This is not a luxury; it's a necessity for sustained progress. Neglecting our physical, mental, and emotional well-being undermines our capacity for growth and resilience. Prioritizing self-care involves engaging in activities that nourish our minds, bodies, and spirits. This could involve regular exercise, mindful eating, adequate sleep, spending time in nature, engaging in creative pursuits, or simply taking time for relaxation and reflection.

The practice of mindfulness can significantly contribute to continuous growth and self-reflection. Mindfulness involves paying attention to the present moment without judgment. By cultivating a mindful awareness, we become more attuned to our thoughts, emotions, and bodily sensations. This awareness allows us to identify patterns of behavior, recognize triggers, and make conscious choices that align with our values and goals. Mindfulness meditation, even for just a few minutes each day, can significantly improve our self-awareness and emotional regulation.

Ultimately, the journey of continuous growth and self-reflection is a lifelong endeavor. It's a path of self-discovery, a process of continually refining our understanding of ourselves and our place in the world. It's not about achieving perfection; it's about embracing the journey, celebrating our progress, and learning from our mistakes. By cultivating a mindset of continuous growth, we create a life that is rich in meaning, purpose, and fulfillment. The path unfolds organically, revealing new facets of ourselves as we navigate the landscape of life.

Embrace the unexpected detours, cherish the small victories, and never stop learning, adapting, and growing. You are on a remarkable journey, and it is one well worth the effort. Embrace the process, celebrate the progress, and trust in the unfolding of your unique and beautiful life.

EMBRACING YOUR AUTHENTIC SELF
THE POWER OF SELF ACCEPTANCE

The journey to your authentic self is a homecoming, a return to the sanctuary of your own soul, where you are finally free to be you.

The journey to a fulfilling life isn't about achieving some idealized version of ourselves, a polished perfection often presented in glossy magazines or social media feeds. It's about embracing the messy, beautiful, and utterly unique individual we already are. Self-acceptance, the cornerstone of authentic living, is the powerful key that unlocks a life filled with purpose, joy, and genuine connection. It's not about ignoring our flaws or pretending they don't exist; it's about acknowledging them, understanding them, and integrating them into the rich complexity of who we are. This isn't a passive acceptance, a resigned shrug of the shoulders. Instead, it's an active, conscious choice to embrace our wholeness – the good, the bad, and the downright ugly.

Many of us have spent years striving for an unattainable ideal, chasing external validation rather than internal peace. We compare ourselves to others, constantly measuring our worth against arbitrary standards set by society, the media, or even our own unrealistic expectations. This constant comparison breeds self-doubt, criticism, and a profound sense of inadequacy. We may achieve significant external success—a prestigious job, a loving family, financial security—yet feel profoundly empty inside. This emptiness stems from a disconnect between our external achievements and our internal reality. Our true selves, our authentic desires and aspirations, remain hidden, stifled by the pressure to conform and meet the expectations of others.

Self-acceptance begins with a radical shift in perspective. We must move away from the critical, judgmental voice in our heads and cultivate a kinder, more compassionate inner dialogue. Imagine treating yourself with the same empathy and understanding you would offer a dear friend struggling with similar challenges. This compassionate self-talk is essential for dismantling the walls of self-criticism that have been built over time. It allows us to see our imperfections not as flaws to be eradicated, but as integral parts of our unique story. Those "flaws," those perceived imperfections, are often the very things that make us relatable, endearing, and uniquely ourselves. They are the fingerprints of our experiences, shaping who we are and lending depth to our character.

The process of self-acceptance isn't a one-time event; it's an ongoing journey, a continuous practice of self-compassion and self-awareness. It requires consistent effort, patience, and a willingness to confront our inner demons. It involves acknowledging our vulnerabilities, accepting our mistakes, and forgiving ourselves for past shortcomings. It's about recognizing that it's okay not to be perfect, that our imperfections don't diminish our worth. Indeed, our imperfections often become our strengths, revealing our resilience, our capacity for growth, and our ability to learn from our experiences.

One powerful tool in the quest for self-acceptance is mindful self-reflection. This involves setting aside dedicated time for quiet introspection, perhaps through journaling, meditation, or simply spending time in nature. By creating space for self-reflection, we can gain a clearer understanding of our thoughts, feelings, and behaviors. We can begin to identify patterns of self-criticism, negative self-talk, and limiting beliefs that are hindering our self-acceptance. Journaling, in particular, can be remarkably effective in this process. By writing down our thoughts and feelings without judgment, we can externalize them, gain perspective, and begin to challenge those negative thought patterns.

Another vital aspect of self-acceptance is cultivating self-compassion. This involves treating ourselves with the same kindness, understanding, and empathy that we would offer a close friend facing difficulties. It's about recognizing that we are all imperfect beings, prone to mistakes and setbacks. S

elf-compassion helps us to navigate these challenges with greater grace and resilience, avoiding self-blame and harsh self-criticism. It involves acknowledging our suffering, offering ourselves reassurance and support, and reminding ourselves that we are not alone in our struggles. This is often easier said than done; it requires conscious practice and a willingness to challenge the ingrained patterns of self-criticism.

Don't seek validation in the mirrors of others. Your worth is found in the unwavering embrace of your authentic self, a reflection of your inner truth.

Building healthy relationships is also intrinsically linked to self-acceptance. When we genuinely accept ourselves, we are better equipped to build authentic and fulfilling relationships with others. We attract people who value us for who we are, flaws and all, fostering deeper, more meaningful connections. These relationships provide support, encouragement, and a sense of belonging, further strengthening our self-acceptance and overall well-being. Conversely, unhealthy relationships can undermine our self-worth and hinder our progress toward self-acceptance. Learning to identify and disengage from such relationships is crucial.

Beyond personal relationships, contributing to something larger than ourselves can be profoundly rewarding and contribute significantly to self-acceptance. Engaging in activities that align with our values, whether it's volunteering, advocating for a cause we believe in, or simply helping a neighbor in need, offers a sense of purpose and connection to something greater than ourselves. This expands our perspective, reminding us that we are part of a larger community and that our individual struggles are shared by others. This sense of shared humanity can be a powerful antidote to feelings of isolation and self-doubt.

The journey to self-acceptance is not without its challenges. There will be moments of doubt, setbacks, and relapses into old patterns of self-criticism. This is perfectly normal and should be met with self-compassion, not self-judgment. The important thing is to keep moving forward, to keep practicing self-compassion, and to keep reminding ourselves of our inherent worth. This continuous self-reflection and practice eventually lead to a deeper sense of self-acceptance and a more fulfilling life.

Remember, self-acceptance is a lifelong process of self-discovery, growth, and unwavering self-compassion.

Embrace the imperfections, celebrate the uniqueness, and acknowledge the inherent worth that lies within you.

The path to a fulfilling life begins with accepting and embracing the magnificent, flawed, beautiful person you are. It's a journey worth taking, one that will lead you to a life of purpose, joy, and genuine connection. The reward is a life lived authentically, a life truly your own. And that, my friends, is a life worth living. The journey may be challenging, but the destination, the feeling of complete self-acceptance, is unparalleled. So embark on this journey with courage, with kindness, and with an unwavering belief in the incredible person you are. The world awaits the authentic you.

Let your authentic self be the compass that guides your life, leading you toward a journey of purpose, passion, and unwavering self-love.

SELF- COMPASSION

Building on the foundation of self-acceptance, we now delve into the vital practice of self-compassion. It's easy to be our own harshest critics, to dwell on our mistakes, and to measure our worth against an unattainable ideal. But what if we approached ourselves with the same kindness and understanding we would offer a dear friend struggling with similar challenges? This is the essence of self-compassion: treating ourselves with the same empathy and grace we extend to others.

Self-compassion isn't self-indulgence or a license for complacency. It's not about ignoring our flaws or avoiding responsibility. Instead, it's about acknowledging our imperfections with a gentle, non-judgmental perspective.

It's recognizing that we are all flawed, that making mistakes is part of the human experience, and that our struggles are not unique. When we stumble, self-compassion allows us to approach our failings with understanding, rather than self-criticism.

Think about a time you offered support to a friend facing hardship. You likely listened without judgment, offered words of encouragement, and reminded them of their strengths. Now, consider extending that same kindness to yourself. When you falter, instead of berating yourself, try offering words of encouragement. Remind yourself of your past successes, your resilience, and your inherent worth.

Cultivating self-compassion is a practice, a skill that requires conscious effort and consistent attention. It's not something that magically appears overnight. It involves actively challenging the negative self-talk that often dominates our inner dialogue. That incessant voice that whispers doubts, criticizes our choices, and magnifies our imperfections needs to be countered with a voice of compassion and understanding.

One effective technique is to engage in mindful self-reflection. Take a moment to pause and observe your thoughts and feelings without judgment. When you notice negative self-talk, gently acknowledge it without getting swept away by it. Imagine you are a compassionate friend witnessing your struggles. What would you say to your friend in this situation? Offer yourself the same words of comfort and encouragement.

Another helpful approach involves practicing self-soothing techniques. When faced with self-criticism, engage in activities that bring you comfort and solace. This could be anything from taking a relaxing bath to listening to calming music, spending time in nature, engaging in a favorite hobby, or practicing mindfulness meditation. The goal is to create a sense of calm and self-nurturing.

Consider keeping a gratitude journal. Every day, write down three things you are grateful for. This simple act can shift your focus from your perceived shortcomings to your blessings, promoting a sense of appreciation and self-worth. It fosters a positive mindset that underpins self-compassion. The gratitude needn't be grand gestures or monumental achievements; appreciating the small things, like a warm cup of tea or a sunny day, can be equally powerful.

Remember that self-compassion isn't about ignoring your mistakes or avoiding responsibility. Instead, it's about learning from your experiences with kindness and understanding. It's about accepting that you're human, that you will make mistakes, and that it's okay to falter along the way. Self-compassion is about choosing to approach your imperfections with gentleness and self-acceptance.

It's crucial to acknowledge that cultivating self-compassion is an ongoing journey, not a destination. There will be times when self-criticism resurfaces, and that's perfectly normal. The key is to gently redirect your thoughts towards self-kindness and understanding. Each time you choose self-compassion over self-criticism, you strengthen your ability to approach life's challenges with greater resilience and inner peace.

Imagine a scenario: You're working on a crucial project, and despite your best efforts, you miss a deadline. Instead of berating yourself with self-criticism ("I'm so incompetent! I'll never succeed!"), try approaching the situation with self-compassion. Acknowledge your disappointment, but also remind yourself that everyone makes mistakes, and that this setback doesn't define your worth or capabilities. Perhaps you'll identify areas for improvement in your time management skills, but do so with a kind, understanding perspective rather than self-condemnation. This gentle approach fosters learning and growth without the self-flagellation that can be so detrimental.

Or consider this: you've been striving to maintain a healthy lifestyle, but you indulged in a less-than-healthy meal. Many would fall into the trap of self-criticism: "I've ruined everything! I'll never reach my goals!" But with self-compassion, the response would be different: "That was a treat, and it's okay to have occasional indulgences. I'll refocus on my healthy eating plan tomorrow." This approach recognizes that setbacks happen, and it's alright to move on without self-recrimination. It allows you to view this incident as an isolated event rather than a sign of personal failure.

Another powerful technique is to use self-compassionate language. Instead of using harsh and critical words like "I should have," "I must," or "I failed," try using kinder, more understanding phrases such as "This is difficult," "I'm doing my best," or "I'm learning and growing." This simple shift in language can significantly impact your internal emotional state. It creates a more supportive and encouraging inner dialogue, fostering self-acceptance and resilience.

Furthermore, consider engaging with others who share similar experiences. This could involve joining a support group, connecting with friends who understand your struggles, or seeking professional guidance from a therapist or counselor. Sharing your experiences with others can help you feel less alone and more understood. Hearing others' stories can help you realize that your imperfections and struggles are not unique, but rather a shared human experience. This shared experience can foster a sense of community and belonging, further strengthening your capacity for self-compassion.

Self-compassion also extends to the realm of physical self-care. Prioritizing your physical health is an act of self-compassion.

This involves regular exercise, nourishing meals, sufficient sleep, and engaging in activities that bring you joy and relaxation. It's about making choices that support your overall well-being, and those choices reflect a deep respect and kindness for your physical and mental health. Remember, you cannot pour from an empty cup; self-compassion necessitates that you first prioritize your own well-being.

It's a reciprocal relationship: as you nurture yourself physically, you strengthen your capacity for emotional self-compassion. When you feel physically strong and healthy, you are better equipped to face life's challenges with resilience and self-acceptance. Conversely, neglecting your physical health can exacerbate negative self-talk and undermine your capacity for self-compassion. It becomes a vicious cycle of self-neglect and self-criticism.

Cultivating self-compassion is an essential step in embracing your authentic self and living a fulfilling life. It's a journey that involves consistent practice, self-awareness, and a conscious shift in perspective. By treating yourself with the same kindness and understanding you would offer a dear friend, you can cultivate a sense of self-acceptance, resilience, and inner peace, ultimately leading to a richer, more meaningful life. Remember that self-compassion isn't a sign of weakness but an undeniable proof of your strength and your willingness to treat yourself with the same kindness and grace you deserve. The rewards are immense – a life lived with greater authenticity, purpose, and joy.

Your authentic self is the purest expression of your soul's song.
Don't silence it; let it resonate with the world, and inspire others to do the same.

BUILDING HEALTHY CONNECTIONS

Embracing our authentic selves isn't a solitary endeavor; it's a journey best shared. While self-compassion forms the bedrock of inner peace, healthy relationships act as the scaffolding, providing support, understanding, and a sense of belonging that amplifies our self-acceptance. These relationships aren't about superficial connections or the pursuit of validation from others; rather, they are authentic bonds built on mutual respect, empathy, and shared growth.

My own journey towards authenticity was profoundly impacted by the relationships I cultivated. For years, I existed in a fog of self-doubt, constantly seeking external validation to compensate for my inner insecurities. My relationships were often turbulent, characterized by codependency and a desperate need for approval. I attracted people who mirrored my own insecurities, creating a cycle of drama and emotional turmoil. Breaking free from this pattern required a conscious effort to redefine my relationships, prioritizing authenticity over the illusion of perfection.

The first step was recognizing the unhealthy patterns. I began journaling, reflecting on my past relationships and identifying recurring themes. I noticed a consistent pattern of choosing partners who needed rescuing, unconsciously reinforcing my own need for significance. This self-awareness was crucial; it illuminated the underlying insecurities fueling my choices and highlighted the need for self-work before I could build healthy relationships.

Self-awareness paved the way for setting healthy boundaries. This wasn't about being selfish; it was about protecting my emotional well-being and fostering relationships where my needs were respected. Learning to say "no" without guilt or explanation was liberating. It freed me from the burden of pleasing others at the expense of my own happiness. It also allowed me to attract people who respected my boundaries, people who valued my autonomy and were interested in a genuine, reciprocal relationship.

Communication, the lifeblood of any healthy relationship, became a focal point. Open, honest communication, free from judgment and defensiveness, allowed me to express my needs and vulnerabilities without fear of rejection. I learned to listen actively, truly hearing what the other person was saying, rather than formulating my response while they were still speaking. These seemingly small changes dramatically improved the quality of my interactions, fostering deeper understanding and trust.

Forgiveness, both of myself and others, was another crucial element. Holding onto resentment and past hurts only perpetuated the cycle of negativity. Forgiving myself for past mistakes allowed me to release the burden of self-blame and move forward with greater compassion. Forgiving others didn't mean condoning their actions; it meant releasing the grip of anger and bitterness, freeing myself from the emotional weight they carried. This process was challenging, requiring patience, self-reflection, and a willingness to let go of the need for retribution.

Choosing the right people to surround myself with became paramount. This wasn't about selecting perfect individuals, but about selecting people who supported my growth, challenged me constructively, and celebrated my authentic self, imperfections and all. I started to prioritize relationships where there was mutual respect, genuine interest in each other's lives, and a shared commitment to personal growth. I found that these relationships, while fewer in number, were infinitely more fulfilling and supportive.

Cultivating healthy relationships isn't about finding the perfect partner or friend; it's about becoming the kind of person who attracts healthy relationships. It's about nurturing those connections with intentionality, honesty, and a commitment to mutual growth. It's about choosing people who lift you up, challenge you to be better, and support your journey towards authenticity.

This journey also involved letting go of relationships that were no longer serving my growth. This is often the most difficult aspect of building healthy relationships, but it's essential for our emotional well-being. Recognizing when a relationship is toxic, whether it's based on codependency, control, or constant negativity, is crucial for our emotional health. Ending these relationships, even though painful, creates space for healthier connections to flourish.

The process isn't always easy. There will be setbacks, moments of doubt, and challenges that test the strength of your relationships. The key is to approach these challenges with self-awareness, compassion, and a commitment to open communication. This isn't about achieving some utopian ideal of perfect relationships; it's about cultivating connections that support your growth, foster your authenticity, and contribute to a more fulfilling life.

Healthy relationships aren't just about romantic partnerships; they encompass the entire spectrum of our connections, from family and friends to colleagues and mentors.

Each relationship holds a unique potential to enrich our lives and contribute to our overall sense of well-being. Investing in these relationships, nurturing them with care, and prioritizing authenticity in our interactions fosters a supportive network that strengthens our sense of belonging and helps us navigate the complexities of life.

Consider, for example, the power of mentorship. A supportive mentor can offer invaluable guidance, encouragement, and a fresh perspective, helping us overcome obstacles and reach our full potential. Mentorship is a reciprocal relationship, offering both the mentor and the mentee opportunities for growth and learning. The mentor gains satisfaction from guiding someone else's development, while the mentee gains access to knowledge, experience, and support. Finding a mentor who aligns with your values and goals can be incredibly transformative.

Similarly, the importance of strong family connections cannot be overstated. While family relationships can be challenging, they often provide a sense of belonging, continuity, and unconditional love that anchors us throughout life. Even when navigating difficult family dynamics, striving for open communication and a willingness to understand different perspectives can foster healthier relationships. Family therapy or counseling can be helpful in navigating complex family situations, providing a structured framework for communication and conflict resolution.

Friendships are essential for emotional support, shared experiences, and a sense of community. True friends provide unconditional love, encouragement, and honest feedback. They celebrate our successes, comfort us in times of hardship, and offer a safe space to express our vulnerabilities. Nurturing friendships requires intentionality – making time for connection, engaging in shared activities, and actively listening to each other's lives.

The path towards building healthy relationships is a continuous process of self-discovery, growth, and learning. It requires a willingness to be vulnerable, to communicate openly, to set healthy boundaries, and to forgive both ourselves and others. It's about recognizing the value of genuine connection, fostering relationships that nourish our souls, and embracing the transformative power of shared experiences. As we embark on this journey, we discover that authentic connections not only enhance our own well-being, but they also enrich the lives of those around us, creating a ripple effect of positivity and mutual growth. The process is iterative, a continuous cycle of self-reflection, learning, and growth. As we become more self-aware, our relationships evolve, reflecting our growth and deepening our sense of belonging. The journey toward authenticity is not a destination, but a lifelong process, and healthy relationships are an integral part of that journey. It's a process of continuous learning, adaptation, and growth, reflecting our evolving understanding of ourselves and our place in the world. The rewards of this continuous effort are profound: a life rich in meaningful connections, a deepened sense of belonging, and a profound understanding of the interconnectedness of life.

CONTRIBUTING TO SOMETHING LARGER THAN YOURSELF

The journey towards embracing our authentic selves isn't solely about inward reflection; it's also about outward expression. It's about discovering how our unique gifts and passions can contribute to something larger than ourselves. This outward focus isn't about seeking external validation; rather, it's about finding purpose and meaning beyond our individual needs and desires. It's about connecting with something greater, something that resonates deeply with our values and aspirations, and in doing so, enriching both our lives and the lives of others.

Think about the moments in your life when you've felt truly alive, truly fulfilled. Were those moments solely focused on personal achievements, or did they involve a connection to something beyond your immediate self? Many of us find our deepest sense of purpose and meaning when we engage in activities that extend beyond our personal ambitions. This could manifest in various ways, from volunteering at a local soup kitchen to advocating for a cause close to our hearts, or even simply offering a helping hand to a neighbor in need.

The act of giving, of contributing to a community, a cause, or even an individual, has a profound impact on our well-being. It shifts our focus from our own internal struggles and anxieties to the needs of others, providing a sense of perspective and purpose. Studies have shown a strong correlation between altruistic behavior and increased levels of happiness and life satisfaction. When we dedicate ourselves to something larger than ourselves, we tap into a wellspring of inner strength and resilience, discovering capacities we never knew we possessed.

This isn't about sacrificing our own happiness for the sake of others; rather, it's about recognizing that our happiness is inextricably linked to the well-being of those around us.

When we contribute to something meaningful, we not only help others, but we also enrich our own lives in countless ways. We gain a sense of belonging, a sense of purpose, and a deeper understanding of our place in the world.

Consider the example of individuals who dedicate their lives to humanitarian work. They often face hardships and challenges, yet they persevere, driven by a profound commitment to their cause. Their actions are a legacy to the power of human compassion and the transformative effect of contributing to something larger than oneself. Their lives are not defined by material possessions or personal achievements, but by the impact they have on the lives of others. Their sense of fulfillment stems not from self-aggrandizement, but from a deep-seated desire to make a positive difference in the world.

Similarly, consider the countless individuals who volunteer their time and energy to local charities and community organizations. They may not receive recognition or reward for their efforts, yet they find immense satisfaction in knowing they're contributing to a greater good. They are building a stronger, more compassionate community, one act of kindness at a time. Their contributions, however small they may seem, have a ripple effect, impacting not only the beneficiaries of their actions but also their own lives in profound ways.

The path towards discovering your contribution doesn't always require grand gestures or sweeping changes. It can begin with small, incremental steps. Perhaps you start by volunteering a few hours a month at a local animal shelter, or by mentoring a young person in your community. Maybe you join a group dedicated to environmental conservation or social justice. The key is to identify a cause that resonates with your values and passions, and to commit yourself to making a difference, however small.

Finding your niche may involve a process of exploration and experimentation. Don't be afraid to try different things, to explore various avenues of involvement until you find something that truly ignites your passion. The process itself is a journey of self-discovery, revealing not only your capacity for compassion and contribution but also your hidden talents and strengths.

Contributing to something larger than ourselves also has a profound impact on our own personal growth. It challenges us to step outside our comfort zones, to confront our fears and insecurities, and to develop new skills and abilities. It forces us to confront our own limitations, to acknowledge our vulnerabilities, and to learn from our mistakes. This process of self-transformation is often unexpected and transformative. It helps us to develop resilience, empathy, and a deeper understanding of the interconnectedness of life.

The journey of self-discovery is not a solitary one. It's a journey that is often enriched and deepened by our connections with others. When we work alongside others for a shared purpose, we discover the power of collaboration and shared experience. We learn to trust, to rely on others, and to celebrate the successes we achieve together. This sense of community and shared purpose is a powerful antidote to feelings of isolation and loneliness.

Moreover, contributing to something larger than ourselves helps us to develop a sense of perspective. When we are immersed in our own challenges and concerns, it is easy to become consumed by them. However, by engaging with the needs of others, we gain a broader perspective on life, recognizing that our own struggles are part of a larger human experience. This perspective helps us to appreciate the importance of compassion, empathy, and understanding.

This isn't simply an act of altruism; it's a pathway to a more fulfilling and meaningful life. The benefits extend far beyond the impact we have on others. It fosters a sense of purpose, strengthens our relationships, and provides us with a sense of belonging. It challenges us to grow, to learn, and to become the best versions of ourselves. It is an investment in our own well-being, a pathway towards living a life that is not only personally enriching but also profoundly meaningful.

As you embark on this journey of contribution, remember that it's a continuous process of learning and growth. There will be setbacks and challenges along the way, but the rewards are immeasurable. The satisfaction of knowing that you have made a positive difference in the world, that you have contributed to something larger than yourself, is a profound and enduring source of fulfillment. This is not merely an act of giving; it's an act of self-discovery, an act of self-acceptance, and ultimately, an act of self-creation. It is a vital component of living a life aligned with our authentic selves. It's about finding our place in the intricate essence of human experience and weaving our unique threads into a richer, more vibrant, and more compassionate world. And in doing so, we discover not only the meaning of life, but also the profound beauty of our own existence. The journey continues, and with each act of contribution, we deepen our understanding of ourselves and our place in the grand scheme of things, weaving a life that is both meaningful and fulfilling. The ripple effect extends beyond our immediate actions, touching the lives of others and shaping a world that reflects our commitment to authenticity and service. Embrace this journey, for it is a path towards a life truly lived.

FULFILLMENT A FINAL REFLECTION

The path towards authenticity isn't a sprint; it's a marathon, a lifelong journey of continuous unveiling and refinement. We are not static beings; we are ever-evolving, shaped by our experiences, our relationships, and our choices. The self we discover today might be subtly, or even dramatically, different from the self we discover tomorrow. That's the beauty, and the challenge, of this ongoing process. Embracing this fluidity, this constant becoming is crucial to living a life of purpose and fulfillment. It's about recognizing that self-discovery is not a destination, but a process of continuous growth and transformation.

Think of it like cultivating a garden. You don't plant a seed and expect a fully grown, blossoming flower overnight. There's weeding, watering, nurturing, and patience involved. Similarly, nurturing our authentic selves requires consistent effort, self-compassion, and a willingness to adapt as we grow and change. There will be moments of doubt, moments of frustration, even moments where we might feel like we're taking steps backward. But these moments are not failures; they are integral parts of the process. They are opportunities for learning, for adjusting our approach, and for deepening our self-awareness.

One of the most significant lessons I've learned on this journey is the importance of forgiveness. Forgiveness, not just of others, but also, and perhaps even more importantly, of ourselves. We all make mistakes, we all stumble, and we all fall short of our ideals from time to time. Holding onto past regrets, harboring self-criticism, and dwelling on our imperfections only hinders our progress. Forgiveness allows us to release the burden of past mistakes, to learn from them, and to move forward with renewed energy and a lighter heart. It's about acknowledging our imperfections while embracing our inherent worthiness.

Another vital aspect of this journey is the cultivation of self-compassion. We are often far more critical of ourselves than we would ever be of someone else. We hold ourselves to impossibly high standards, expecting perfection where it's simply unattainable. Self-compassion, on the other hand, involves treating ourselves with the same kindness, understanding, and acceptance that we would offer a dear friend. It's about recognizing our vulnerabilities, acknowledging our struggles, and offering ourselves the grace and support we need to navigate life's challenges.

The journey towards authenticity is also inextricably linked to our relationships with others. Our interactions with family, friends, colleagues, and even strangers shape our understanding of ourselves and the world. These relationships provide opportunities for growth, for learning, and for deepening our self-awareness. They challenge us, support us, and help us to see ourselves through different lenses. Authentic relationships, based on trust, respect, and mutual understanding, are invaluable in our quest for self-discovery. They provide a safe space for vulnerability, for self-expression, and for the exploration of our deepest selves. Investing in these relationships is an act of self-care, a confirmation of our commitment to our own well-being and growth.

Living a life of purpose often involves stepping outside of our comfort zones. It means embracing challenges, taking risks, and venturing into the unknown. It's about pushing our boundaries, expanding our horizons, and discovering what we are truly capable of achieving.

This might involve pursuing a long-held dream, making a significant career change, or simply saying "yes" to opportunities that once seemed daunting. Each time we step outside of our comfort zones, we grow, we learn, and we deepen our understanding of ourselves and our capabilities.

But what does a life of purpose actually look like? It's not necessarily about achieving a specific goal or accumulating wealth. It's about living a life that aligns with our values, our passions, and our deepest sense of self. It's about making a contribution to the world, however small, and finding meaning and fulfillment in our daily lives. For some, it might involve pursuing a creative passion, like painting, writing, or music. For others, it might be about serving others through volunteering or activism. For still others, it might involve simply being present for loved ones, offering support and companionship. The definition of purpose is unique to each individual. There is no one-size-fits-all answer, and that's precisely the point.

The journey of self-discovery is often intertwined with confronting our fears. Fear can be a powerful inhibitor, holding us back from pursuing our dreams and living authentically. But fear is not an insurmountable obstacle. It's a feeling, an emotion, and like all emotions, it is temporary.

By acknowledging our fears, understanding their origins, and gradually confronting them, we can break free from their grip and create a life that is more aligned with our desires. This process often involves small, incremental steps, starting with manageable challenges and gradually increasing the level of difficulty as our confidence grows. The key is to approach each challenge with courage, self-compassion, and a belief in our own capacity to overcome.

Another crucial component of living a fulfilling life is the acceptance of our imperfections. We are not perfect beings; we are flawed, complex, and multifaceted. We make mistakes, we have shortcomings, and we fall short of our ideals from time to time. But these imperfections are not flaws; they are part of what makes us unique, interesting, and ultimately, human.

Embracing our imperfections means acknowledging our vulnerabilities, accepting our limitations, and learning to love ourselves unconditionally. It's about celebrating our uniqueness, rather than striving for an unattainable ideal of perfection.

The journey towards living a fulfilling life is a continuous process of growth and self-discovery. It requires courage, resilience, self-compassion, and a willingness to embrace the unknown.

It involves confronting our fears, accepting our imperfections, and nurturing our authentic selves. But the rewards are immeasurable. The ability to live a life that aligns with our values, passions, and deepest sense of self brings a level of peace, joy, and fulfillment that is simply unparalleled. It's a life lived with purpose, meaning, and a profound sense of connection to something larger than ourselves. It's a life truly lived, a life deeply and authentically ours.

This journey requires consistent introspection. Regularly ask yourself: What brings me joy? What are my values? What kind of impact do I want to make on the world? What are my strengths and weaknesses? Honest answers to these questions provide a compass to guide you on your path. Journaling, meditation, and spending time in nature can be incredibly helpful tools for self-reflection. These practices provide a space for introspection, allowing you to connect with your inner wisdom and gain a deeper understanding of your authentic self.

It's also crucial to remember that this journey is personal. There is no one-size-fits-all approach to finding your purpose or living a fulfilling life. What works for one person might not work for another. The most important thing is to be true to yourself, to listen to your inner voice, and to trust your intuition.

Don't compare your journey to others; focus on your own path, your own pace, and your own unique expression of authenticity.

Remember the moments of doubt, the challenges overcome, the lessons learned – they are the threads that weave the rich essence of your life.

Each experience, both positive and negative, contributes to your growth and understanding. Embrace these experiences, learn from them, and allow them to shape you into the person you are meant to be. The journey towards authenticity is a continuous evolution, a lifelong process of self-discovery and transformation. It is a path filled with joy, sorrow, growth, and ultimately, profound fulfillment.

And finally, remember the power of gratitude. Take time each day to appreciate the good things in your life, both big and small. Cultivate a sense of thankfulness for the people in your life, for your health, for your opportunities, and for the simple joys of everyday existence. Gratitude shifts your perspective, allowing you to focus on the positive aspects of your life and to appreciate the abundance that surrounds you. It is a powerful tool for cultivating joy, contentment, and a deep sense of inner peace. It strengthens your resilience and enhances your capacity for happiness. It allows you to approach life's challenges with a sense of perspective and gratitude for the journey itself.

The pursuit of a fulfilling life is not a destination, but a continuous journey of self-discovery, growth, and contribution.

It's a process of embracing our authentic selves, connecting with our purpose, and making a positive impact on the world. May this journey be filled with joy, meaning, and a deep sense of self-acceptance. May you discover the unique beauty and potential within yourself and live a life that is both meaningful and profoundly fulfilling.

Don't seek validation in the mirrors of others. Your worth is found in the unwavering embrace of your authentic self, a reflection of your inner truth.

THE ALCHEMIST WITHIN

FORGING GOLD FROM THE LEAD OF SELF

We are all, in essence, alchemists. Not chasing the mythical philosopher's stone to transmute base metals into gold, but embarking on a far more profound and personal journey: the alchemy of self-discovery. This is not a passive observation, a gentle unraveling, but a fiery, passionate, and often painful process of burning away the dross, chiseling away the impurities, and ultimately forging a self sculpted from the raw material of experience, vulnerability, and unwavering self-compassion.

The journey begins with a spark — a disquiet within, a sense that we are not quite living the life we were meant to. This ember, often ignited by hardship, disappointment, or simply the quiet whisper of our soul, is the first call to adventure. It urges us to look inward, to confront the narratives we've been told, the expectations we've adopted, and the masks we've carefully crafted to navigate the world. It is the moment we acknowledge that the lead of our conditioned self, heavy with fear and self-doubt, needs to be transmuted. In this initial flicker of awareness, a seed of possibility is planted, a yearning for something more authentic, more aligned with the essence of who we truly are. It is a courageous step, a willingness to question the very foundations upon which we have built our lives.

And what a fearsome process it can be! Self-discovery is not a gentle stroll through a blooming garden. It's a descent into the shadowy corners of our psyche, a confrontation with the demons we've long suppressed. It requires courage, a willingness to feel the sting of past hurts, the ache of unfulfilled dreams, and the burning shame of perceived failures. This is the crucible, the fiery furnace where our old selves are tested, refined, and ultimately purified. We may encounter the ghosts of past traumas, the echoes of critical voices, and the weight of societal pressures that have shaped our beliefs and behaviors. This internal excavation can be unsettling, even terrifying, as we unearth aspects of ourselves that we have long sought to bury. Yet, it is in this very act of facing our shadows that we begin to reclaim our power and pave the way for genuine transformation.

But the heat is not meant to destroy; it is meant to reveal. Just as a goldsmith uses fire to melt away the impurities in gold ore, so too does the struggle of self-discovery expose the inherent brilliance within us. In the heart of the pain, we discover our resilience, our capacity for empathy, and our unwavering spirit to overcome. We begin to understand that our imperfections are not blemishes, but rather the unique markings that make us who we are. These scars, these imperfections, become evidences to our strength, our ability to heal, and our willingness to embrace the totality of our human experience. They are what makes us unique, what distinguishes us from the faceless masses, and what ultimately contributes to the richness and complexity of our character.

The process is not solitary. We need mentors, guides, and fellow travelers who have walked this path before. We need the support of friends and family who can hold space for our vulnerability and celebrate our small victories. We need to immerse ourselves in wisdom – through books, music, art, and the profound teachings of nature – to gain different perspectives and find solace in the shared human experience. Surrounding ourselves with those who uplift and inspire us, who challenge our limiting beliefs, and who offer unconditional support is essential for navigating the often turbulent waters of self-discovery. These connections serve as anchors, reminding us that we are not alone in our struggles and that there is always hope for a brighter future.

This is not a race to be won, but a dance to be danced. There are moments of exhilarating clarity, where we feel a surge of understanding, a moment of profound connection to our true selves. But there are also moments of doubt, of despair, when we feel lost and uncertain. The key is to embrace the ebb and flow, to be patient with ourselves, and to trust that the process, however challenging, is ultimately leading us to a place of greater authenticity and self-acceptance. Self-compassion becomes our guiding principle, allowing us to treat ourselves with the same kindness and understanding that we would offer a dear friend. Recognizing that setbacks are inevitable and that progress is not always linear, we learn to forgive ourselves for our mistakes and to celebrate our small victories along the way.

The gold, the culmination of this alchemical journey, is not a fixed entity, a perfect and unchanging version of ourselves. It is a fluid, evolving state of being. It is the ability to live with intention, to make choices that are aligned with our values, to embrace our vulnerability, and to show up in the world with genuine compassion and unwavering self-love. It is the realization that we are not defined by our past, but empowered by it. This "gold" is not a destination but a continuous process of refinement, a deepening understanding of ourselves and our place in the world. It is the ability to navigate life's challenges with grace, resilience, and an unwavering commitment to living a life that is both meaningful and fulfilling.

The alchemy of self-discovery is a lifelong pursuit, a continuous process of learning, growing, and evolving. It requires dedication, perseverance, and an unwavering belief in our potential. But the rewards are immeasurable. For in the end, the gold we forge is not just a more refined version of ourselves, but a life lived with purpose, passion, and a profound sense of inner peace. It is a life where we are no longer driven by fear and self-doubt but by love, compassion, and a deep sense of connection to something greater than ourselves. So, embrace the fire, confront your demons, and embark on your own alchemical journey. The world awaits the gold you are destined to become, the unique and radiant expression of your true self that is waiting to be unveiled. Let the transformative power of self-discovery guide you towards a life of authenticity, purpose, and boundless joy.

SCULPTING THE MASTERPIECE
OF SELF

We are ushered into existence amidst a symphony of possibilities, a vast, uncharted canvas eagerly awaiting the first, tentative stroke of our brush. Unlike a preordained painting or a meticulously planned sculpture, the masterpiece we are destined to become is not etched in the stars or dictated by the whims of fate. Instead, it is a living, breathing creation, meticulously sculpted from the raw materials of experience, painstakingly chiseled by the deliberate choices we make, and brought to vibrant life by the unwavering, incandescent flame of unwavering self-belief. We are, in essence, the architects of our own becoming, entrusted with the profound and exhilarating power to design the life we yearn to inhabit.

This realization is not merely a comforting platitude to soothe our anxieties; it is a deeply resonant philosophical truth that has reverberated through the corridors of time, captivating thinkers and inspiring generations. From the existentialist philosophers who championed the radical freedom of individual choice to the contemporary motivational speakers who ignite the dormant spark of potential within the human heart, the core message echoes with unwavering clarity: we are not mere passive recipients of life's capricious events, but rather active, engaged participants in their unfolding. We are the authors of our own compelling narratives, the composers of our unique and soul-stirring melodies, the directors of our own captivating dramas, each scene brimming with possibility.

This extraordinary power, however, is not a magical amulet, a readily available shortcut to effortless success. It demands conscious, unwavering effort, resolute dedication, and a heartfelt, unyielding commitment to the often-challenging journey of self-discovery. It requires us to delve into the deepest recesses of our being, to examine our strengths and weaknesses with unflinching honesty and disarming vulnerability, and to identify the core values that will serve as our guiding stars, illuminating the path ahead and informing our most crucial decisions. It is a lifelong odyssey of continuous learning, profound self-reflection, and courageous reinvention, a constant process of refining and redefining who we are and who we aspire to be.

In the intricate and nuanced art of self-creation, we are inevitably bound to encounter a myriad of challenges, disheartening setbacks, and fleeting moments of self-doubt that threaten to derail our progress. But these trials are not omens of impending failure; they are, in reality, invaluable opportunities for profound growth, for cultivating resilience in the face of adversity, and for forging a deeper, more nuanced understanding of ourselves and our capabilities. Like the refiner's fire that purifies gold, these challenges have the potential to transform us into stronger, more resilient versions of ourselves.

The true key to navigating these turbulent waters lies in recognizing the transformative power of perspective, the ability to shift our gaze and reframe our experiences. We possess the inherent capacity to choose to perceive obstacles as insurmountable walls that block our path, or as strategically placed stepping stones that propel us toward higher ground, toward greater heights of personal and professional fulfillment. We can choose to dwell on our past mistakes, allowing them to fester and define us, or we can choose to learn from them, extracting valuable wisdom and using that knowledge to forge a brighter, more promising future. We can choose to succumb to the paralyzing grip of fear and the insidious allure of mediocrity, or we can choose to embrace our boundless potential and bravely strive for greatness, refusing to settle for anything less than our best selves. The choice, ultimately and irrevocably, is ours to make.

This transformative journey of self-sculpting is rarely, if ever, easy, demanding unwavering self-compassion, especially when we are confronted with the sting of adversity and the weight of our own imperfections. It demands that we learn to silence the relentless inner critic, that harsh voice that delights in pointing out our flaws and undermining our confidence, and instead cultivate a nurturing voice of encouragement and unwavering self-belief, a voice that reminds us of our inherent worth and our capacity for greatness. It also necessitates surrounding ourselves with supportive individuals who genuinely believe in our potential, who uplift us during times of doubt, and who inspire us to reach for the stars, to chase our dreams with unwavering passion and unyielding determination.

But the rewards of embarking on this profound and transformative journey are truly immeasurable, far exceeding any sacrifices we may make along the way. To witness the gradual unfolding of our potential, to see our long-cherished dreams slowly but surely take shape before our very eyes, to live a life authentically aligned with our deepest values and our most cherished aspirations, is a deeply profound and profoundly fulfilling experience. It is to truly understand the profound meaning of self-empowerment, to recognize the inherent power that resides within each Ada every one of us, and to embrace the boundless possibilities that lie dormant, waiting to be awakened and unleashed upon the world.

Let us, therefore, wholeheartedly embrace the role of the architect within, the creative force that has the power to shape our destinies. Let us dare to dream audaciously, to take calculated risks that push us beyond our comfort zones, and to never cease learning and growing, constantly expanding our horizons and refining our skills. Let us approach the canvas of our lives with unwavering passion, with a clear sense of purpose, and with the unshakeable belief that we possess the inherent power to sculpt ourselves into the masterpiece we were always meant to be. For in the end, the most inspiring and heartfelt creation we will ever undertake is the creation of our own authentic, fulfilling, and extraordinary self, a proof to the power of human potential. The power is within you, waiting to be unleashed. Now, go forth and create!

The journey of sculpting the masterpiece of self is not a swift stroke, but a patient, deliberate dance with time. Each challenge faced, each lesson learned, is a gentle tap of the chisel, revealing the intricate contours of your evolving soul. Embrace the slow, steady process, for the most profound beauty emerges from the depths of patient transformation.

*Do not be afraid of the rough edges, the
seemingly unrefined aspects of your being.
They are the raw materials from which your
masterpiece will emerge.
Like a sculptor who sees the form within the
stone, learn to see the potential within yourself,
and with unwavering intent, carve away
the unnecessary, revealing the true
essence of your spirit.*

www.ingramcontent.com/pod-product-compliance
Lightning Source LLC
Chambersburg PA
CBHW041202150726

48006CB00016B/2084